Inside Academic Writing

Understanding Audience and Becoming Part of an Academic Community

Grace Canseco

Ann Arbor
University of Michigan Press

Published in the United States of America
The University of Michigan Press
Manufactured in the United States of America

∞ Printed on acid-free paper

ISBN-13: 978-0-472-03389-8

2013 2012 2011 2010 4 3 2 1

Acknowledgments

I would like to recognize and thank the individuals at Emory University who allowed me to use their writings in the textbook.

Daniel Domingues da Silva, Fernando Esquivel Suarez, Oksana Gomas, Anthony Luyai, Dr. Alberto Moreno, Dr. Rosa Morra, Dr. Jim Nagy, Duc Bui Nguyen, Margarita Pintado Burgos, Anastasia Valecce, Hengbin Wang, and Chunfu Xu.

I would also like to acknowledge authors whose textbooks and ideas have guided me throughout my teaching career.

Braine, George, and Claire May. (1996.) *Writing from Sources: A Guide for ESL Students*. Mountain View, CA: Mayfield Publishing Company.

Byrd, Patricia, and Beverly Benson. (1989.) *Improving the Grammar of Written English: The Handbook*. Belmont, CA: Wadsworth Publishing Company.

Byrd, Patricia, and Beverly Benson. (1994.) *Problem/Solution: A Reference for ESL Writers*. Boston: Heinle & Heinle Publishers.

Dollahite, Nancy E., and Julie Haun. (2006.) *Sourcework: Academic Writing from Sources*. Boston: Thomson Heinle.

Flowerdew, John, and Matthew Peacock. (2001.) *Research Perspectives on English for Academic Purposes*. Cambridge, UK: Cambridge University Press.

Gawande, Atul. (2006.) *The Best American Science Writing*. New York: Harper Collins Publishers.

Graff, Gerald, and Cathy Birkenstein. (2006.) *They Say/I Say: The Moves that Matter in Academic Writing*. New York: Norton & Company.

Hinkel, Eli. (2004.) *Teaching Academic ESL Writing*, Mahwah, NJ: Lawrence Erlbaum.

Johns, Ann. M. (1997.) *Text, Role and Context*. Cambridge, UK: Cambridge University Press.

Kroll, Barbara. (1990.) *Second Language Writing: Research Insights for the Classroom*. Cambridge, UK: Cambridge University Press.

Menasche, Lionel. (1997.) *Writing a Research Paper, Rev. Ed.* Ann Arbor: University of Michigan Press.

Raimes, Ann. (1996.) *Keys for Writers: A Brief Handbook*. Boston: Houghton Mifflin Company.

Swales, John M., and Christine B. Feak. (2000.) *English in Today's Research World*. Ann Arbor: University of Michigan Press.

Swales, John M., and Christine B. Feak. (2004.) *Academic Writing for Graduate Students: Essential Tasks and Skills, Second Edition*. Ann Arbor: University of Michigan Press.

Weissberg, Robert, and Suzanne Buker. (1990.) *Writing Up Research: Experimental Research Report Writing for Students of English*. Englewood Cliffs, NJ: Prentice Hall Regents.

Williams, James D. (2001.) *The LEA Guide to Composition*. Mahwah, NJ: Lawrence Erlbaum.

Williams, James D. (2003.) *Preparing to Teach Writing: Research, Theory and Practice, Third Edition*. Mahwah, NJ: Lawrence Erlbaum.

To My Students:

I appreciate and honor all the students in my academic writing classes over the years at Emory University. Your enthusiasm and willingness to apply the principles of academic writing to your program assignments, grants, travel fellowships, publications, and dissertations have truly inspired me. You often began with a bit of fear and finished with confidence and success. To all of you, I owe a very special thank you! In particular, I wish to congratulate and thank *Daniel Domingues da Silva* and *Ana Diaz Gomez*! I will never forget you!

To Julianne Chung:

I respect your young, relentless energy and enthusiasm for writing to reach all audiences about your research interest. If you could be cloned, we would have perfect students!

To Peggy Wagner:

No words can describe my gratitude to you for the endless hours of brainstorming, creating, and developing materials with me for our writing classes since the very beginning of the program. Your creativity and energy bounces off the walls to keep me going! It seems I have learned from you forever!

To Jennifer Greer:

Thank you, my "wordsmither," for your relentless and vigorous support. When I was weary and disillusioned, you cheered me up. When I couldn't find a word or an idea, you gave me one. You made it happen!

To My ESL Colleagues:

My admiration and appreciation extend to Alan Forsyth, Grace Song, and Heather Boldt who have worked tirelessly as a team to guide our student writers. Thank you!

To Kelly Sippell:

Thank you, Kelly, for your patience, encouragement, and belief in me.

To Julio:

For your love and support!

Grateful acknowledgment is given to the following authors, publishers, and journals for granting permission to reprint previously published materials.

The Chronicle of Higher Education for "Review blasts professors for plagiarism by graduate student" by Paula Wasley, Volume 52, Issue 41, Page A13 © 2006.

Lawrence Erlbaum for excerpts from *Teaching Academic ESL Writing: Practical Techniques in Vocabulary and Grammar* by Eli Hinkel. Copyright © 2004. [pending]

Macmillan Publishers, Ltd. for "In vivo cancer targeting and imaging with semiconductor quantum dots" by Xiohu Gao et al., *Nature Biotechnology,* Volume 22, No. 8, August 2004 © 2004 Nature Publishing Group; "Turning a blind eye," *Nature Medicine,* Volume 14, No. 1 January 2008 © 2008 Nature Publishing Group; "Darwin 200: Should scientists study race and IQ? NO" by Stephen Rose, *Nature,* Vol. 457 © 2009 Nature Publishing Group; "Darwin 200: Should scientists study race and IQ? YES by Stephen Ceci and Wendy M. Williams, *Nature* 457 © 2009 Nature Publishing Group.

ScienceDaily.com for "Boys' and girls' brains are different: Gender differences in language appear biological," *ScienceDaily* 5 March 2008. 27 October 2009, www.sciencedaily.com /releases/2008/03/080303120346.htm; "Fussy baby? Linking genes, brain and behavior in children," *Science Daily,* www.sciencedaily.com /releases/2009/07/090713114501.htm; "Bottoms up: Individualists more likely to be problem drinkers." *ScienceDaily* 21 November 2008. 27 October 2009, www.sciencedaily.com /releases/2008/11/081117121235.htm.

Every effort has been made to contact the copyright holders for permissions to reprint borrowed material. We regret any oversights that may have occurred and will rectify them in future printings of this book.

Contents

To the Instructor

"The moment we write we become part of a writing community. Do we do it as insiders or outsiders?"

—Arthur Brooks and Peter Grundy, 1990,
Writing for Study Purposes: A Teacher's Guide to Developing Individual Writing Skills
(Cambridge University Press)

With the growing numbers of graduate students and the importance of writing for coursework, conferences, and publication, a need for writing textbooks has also grown. Many universities have started offering courses designed for undergraduates desiring a graduate career or for new graduate students who haven't had the training needed for success in an academic graduate program.

While other textbooks prepare students for graduate writing and assume prior knowledge or training, few textbooks bridge the gap between non-academic writing and more academic texts—the difference between being outside the academic community and inside with peers, colleagues, and experts in the same field.

Inside Academic Writing gives students the opportunity to examine basic assumptions about writing before proceeding to teach students to target their audience and map the flow of information. It allows students to think about the readers of their texts so that they develop a better piece of writing.

Throughout, students create a portfolio of pieces such as a biographical statement and a research interest essay—pieces that are important to many types of writing but that are rarely taught. So often, students are taught about the parts of a research grant, a fellowship application, or a conference paper, but rarely are they taught how to develop the pieces about themselves.

Inside Academic Writing is a predecessor to graduate-level writing. Its personal nature will help students create writings that they'll use outside the classroom—writings they really need. Students preparing for future academic study in any discipline can focus on whether the grammar is correct but also on the writing as a whole—is it the correct piece for the purpose it is to serve? In other words, depending on the purpose of the writing and who it is for, students can determine on their own who the audience is and if they've written an appropriate piece.

Inside Academic Writing is designed to help students cope with the challenges of developing materials for grants, fellowships, conferences, and publication. The crux of the writing is taught in academic writing courses, but the reasons why we write what we do and the ways to adapt the writings for different audiences are not. Created as a predecessor to other academic writing texts, the goal of *Inside Academic Writing* is to give students the chance to create words for a variety of audiences and the knowledge necessary to recognize the difference in audience.

While giving an overview of grammar, *Inside Academic Writing* minimizes students' time by having them create a portfolio of writings they'll be able to use and adapt long after they've left the classroom.

Inside Academic Writing addresses the needs of students whose first language is not English as they begin to position themselves as skilled writers in their fields of study, research, and professions. The textbook assumes that these students have an intermediate to low-advanced level of grammar from previous courses or from having prepared for the TOEFL®, GRE®, GMAT®, and/or other standardized English tests. They have probably memorized long lists of vocabulary and learned the verb tenses (including active and passive voice), the parts of speech, and the rules for punctuation; however, they generally do not apply them consistently in academic writing or adapt each writing text for a particular audience or academic genre. Therefore, this textbook offers samples for students to read and others for them to analyze before applying the concepts and strategies to the writing assignments.

Inside Academic Writing situates students within their writing communities quickly and easily by prioritizing the steps of learning. Students are not presented all grammar rules and all genres of academic writing but are directed to use the common threads of academic writing across disciplines. Students are encouraged to write about topics related to their field of study for both general academic readers and for others in their field or their lab partners.

The first part of the textbook presents the distinctiveness of academic writing for English-speaking readers, the second incorporates practice strategies and techniques, and the third guides students to create common texts and structures.

The text is divided into ten units that fall into three parts. Part 1 contains three units that introduce students to the world of academic writing. Students are given an overview of concepts needed to view their writing as a whole—they learn to target an audience, use academic language, develop paragraphs, and then incorporate cohesive devices to make sure each paragraph flows into the next all the while not straying from the claim or thesis or losing sight of reader expectations. Part 2 focuses on strategies for the actual writing experience—using outside sources, planning, drafting, evaluating, and editing. Part 3 introduces several structural formats students can use while reinforcing the concepts and strategies used in Parts 1 and 2.

Each writing assignment is specific to the student and his or her field; students are required to search for sources, use vocabulary, and incorporate ideas specific to their fields of study. By completing the textbook, students will have a substantial portfolio of writings including a biographical statement, a research interest essay, and several papers that could be used for assignments and publications within their fields both during their academic career and well into their professional career.

This textbook includes grading criteria and rubrics for students as they progress through the chapters and writing tasks with the tools to emerge as skilled academic writers. Grading criteria and rubrics are conveniently placed as appendixes at the back of the textbook. Students reflect on their growth as writers while developing a writing portfolio that illustrates what they are learning, their strengths and weaknesses, and the problems they are facing.

This textbook is designed primarily for students whose second language is English and for courses where students are being prepared for academic graduate writing. Sample writings are taken from a variety of disciplines and offer ample opportunity for students to read, analyze, and edit for the concepts taught in the textbook. By doing so, students can then apply the concepts to their own writings. Depending on the length of the course, there may be more material than can be covered during the class. Exercises need not be done in the order they appear in the text. Also, instructors may want to repeat certain exercises by having students find and analyze articles or readings written by professors and/or experts in their own fields. Many of the exercises can be assigned as homework; those assignments can then be collected for grading or discussed in small groups or as part of a class discussion. Materials for the teacher can be found online at www.press.umich.edu/esl/.

To the Student

"What is written without effort is read in general without pleasure."

—Samuel Johnson, author, critic,
and lexicographer (1709–1784)

Inside Academic Writing sets priorities for learning to help you build a solid foundation of writing standards, strategies, and skills to become a successful writer in the academic community. The writing assignments required of you will vary by fields of study, but the primary qualities of clear writing across disciplines will remain the same. How well you master these qualities expected by English-speaking, academic readers will determine whether you write as an *insider or an outsider.*

Few skills will be as important to you as a graduate student and professional scholar as writing. To be recognized as a member of an academic community, you must write purposefully and correctly, which requires effort. You will need to write for readers who share your field of study and also for readers who do not understand the technical and specific aspects of your field. Writing for colleagues in your field may not seem difficult to you while writing for general academics will challenge you. You may question the importance or relevance of learning to "tell the story" of your research interests and ideas in a convincing and novel manner to the general public; however, the best research ideas have little value unless they are understood by your professors, grant review committees, and interested individuals and agencies that work to implement them. Writing well for a broad audience will help you compete for recognition with other students and researchers and provide you with opportunities for fellowship and grant support from universities and funding agencies to complete your research projects. In short, the ability to write for experts and non-experts will give you a competitive advantage.

Inside Academic Writing:

- emphasizes the importance of writing communities and the underlying assumptions of English-speaking writers as well as the accepted conventions and standards in discipline-specific writing communities
- presents the basic qualities of writing expected by writers in U.S. academic settings
- targets learning strategies to help you write easier, faster, and smarter
- provides a variety of tasks to practice the skills needed to become credible writers in your fields and future professions
- highlights the need for you to synthesize and document information without plagiarizing
- focuses on individual learning by helping you target specific areas most critical to your advancement
- directs you to evaluate, revise, edit, and proofread your individual writings
- guides you to create a portfolio or collection of your writings to reflect on your progress

By developing the learning strategies, skills, and structures in this textbook, you will begin to position yourself as a respected member of a scholarly community.

Welcome to the world of academic writing!

Grading Criteria

The grading criteria and rubrics contain the components expected in academic writing and will direct you in analyzing and evaluating your writing assignments. By visualizing your strengths and weaknesses based on the rubrics, you begin to develop your own academic writing profile and learn to improve your skills. The grading criteria and rubrics are located in the Appendixes that begin on page 178.

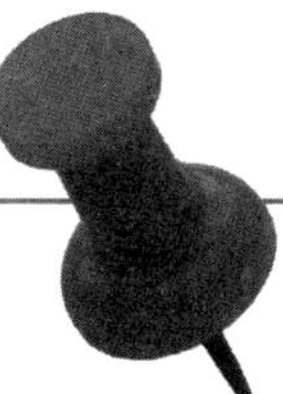

Part 1

Understanding Academic Writing

UNIT 1

Writing Communities: Insider or Outsider?

"A good writer is like a well-mannered person; s/he is considerate of others. S/he must know who her/his readers or listeners are and aim, with this in mind, for the most rapid and comfortable communication possible."

—*Scientific Writing for Graduate Students*
(Council of Biology Editors, Inc.)

Writing in academic and professional settings positions you in a variety of communities with common features. First, you become a member of a broad U.S. academic community of writers in a range of fields. These writers generally share basic assumptions or beliefs about the qualities of effective writing that might be different from the assumptions in other countries. For example, in the United States, the responsibility for communicating clearly belongs to the writer, but in some countries it might rest with the reader. Second, you join smaller target communities—your academic program, research group, and university/professional organizations—that use varied features and conventions that you will need to understand. This unit will help you examine the **basic assumptions** of academic writers, how to **target your audience,** and the use of **academic language**. By analyzing these concepts and creating a brief research interest statement for two types of audiences, you will take your first step into the university writing community.

Basic Assumptions

You have probably already developed a set of assumptions and beliefs about effective writing. Some of these may be similar or different from the basic assumptions accepted across disciplines at an English-speaking university. Think about the assumptions you bring from your experience in three areas: audience (Who are your readers?), purpose (How should you make a claim or thesis?), and organization (How should you order your text?). Share them with a classmate (preferably someone in a different field of study), and list them.

Audience:

Purpose:

Organization:

Exercise 1A: Understanding Assumptions of Academic Writers

Complete this survey to compare your beliefs with a skilled academic writer's assumptions. Circle T for true or F for false according to your expectations about writing.

1. The main purpose of an academic writing is stated clearly and explicitly near the beginning of the text. T F
2. The reader should never have to guess the meaning of the writer. T F
3. It is important to tell the reader what is going to be written about, to write about it, and then to rephrase it at the end of the text. T F
4. The organization of the writing should be well mapped and organized so that the reader can visualize it easily. T F
5. A reader expects to find credible and relevant details to support general statements. T F
6. The main point of the writing should be reaffirmed and repeated frequently throughout the text. T F
7. A writer usually starts with a generalization and moves to specific details to support this generalization. T F
8. The main idea of a paragraph should be shown with topic sentences at the beginning of each paragraph. T F
9. Formal language should always be used in academic writing. T F

10. Good grammar is required.  F
11. "Ownership" of the written word is important. A writer must give credit to the owner in the form of footnotes and citations for words that are paraphrased or summarized.  F
12. Academic writing is usually persuasive, presenting a unique perspective and claim. 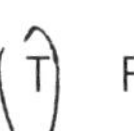 F

If you answered true to all the questions in this survey of assumptions, you share the general assumptions of English-speaking academic writers. Mark the ones that you answered as false, and ask your instructor to explain the assumptions.

Exercise 1B: Free Writing and Understanding Assumptions

To organize your thoughts on assumptions and how you might need to adapt your views, try free writing for 10 minutes describing one of your assumptions that differs from one of the basic beliefs in Exercise 1A.

1. Put your thoughts on paper as quickly as possible. (This is free writing.)
2. Stop and read your thoughts.
3. Mark one or two ways that differ from the assumption you selected.
4. Write one sentence describing the assumption you want to acquire.

Targeting Your Audience

Understanding and learning to direct your ideas to different English-speaking readers may well be one of your most difficult and critical challenges as a writer. Just as we adjust our speech when we talk to professors, friends, grandparents, or strangers to appear well-mannered and polite, we must also alter or modify our writing for different readers (even those within our field of study). For example, a chemist writing for the journal *Science* (a popular magazine for a general academic audience) will include background information, definitions, examples, and explanations for a **general (non-expert) reader (GR)** who is probably interested in the human aspect of the research. However, writing for a field-specific publication such as *The Journal of Mass Spectrometry*, a chemist will use specialized and technical vocabulary and will omit general definitions and explanations because a **field expert reader (FER)** understands the concepts and shares a background of information with the writer. You will write for both types of readers but primarily for professors inside or outside of your department and for general readers outside of the university when you apply for research grants or fellowships. Some of you might even publish your student research ideas in academic journals, alumni and student magazines, local newspapers, or on department web pages. The **audience or reader chart** (Figure 1) can help you visualize your current role as a writer among GRs and FERs.

Figure 1: Audience or Reader Chart

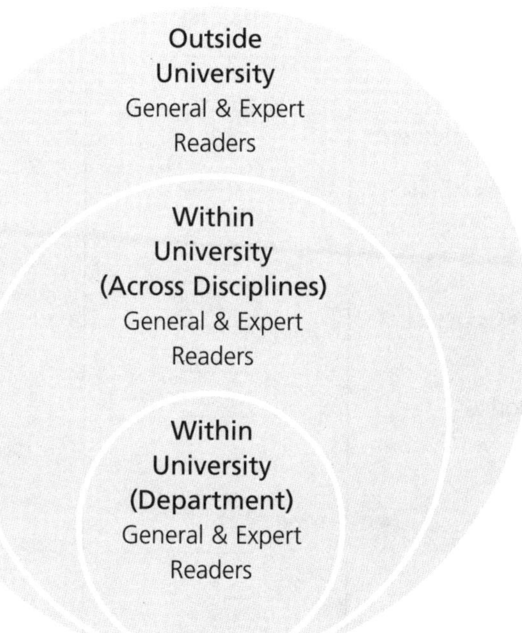

To target a GR or an FER you should:

1. Determine if the readers share or do not share your knowledge about the topic.
2. Select appropriate vocabulary and language for the type of reader.
3. Organize the text with the conventions expected by the type of readers.

Exercise 1C: Considering Readers

Evaluate the common academic types of texts listed by considering the possible readers. Indicate whether the text would primarily have Audience 1 or Audience 2. In some cases, the text may have both types of audiences.

Audience 1. General Readers (GRs)

Audience 2. Field Expert Readers (FERs)

Type	Reader
Abstract	______
Biographic statement	______
Cover letter	______
Thesis	______
Email	______
Academic essay	______
Grant	______
Lab report	______
Resume	______
Proposal	
☐ conference	______
☐ dissertation	______
Published article	______

Exercise 1D: Selecting an Area of Interest for General Readers

Select a developing research area related to your field of study (or one that interests you). Later you will write a paragraph about this developing area to share with GRs.

1. Write your area of interest here. ______________________
2. Why do you believe GRs will be interested in this area?

____

____

____

Language Choice

An obvious and important difference between texts written for GRs and FERs is the vocabulary. Compare the sample sentences from the articles in the same field: *In vivo cancer targeting and imaging with semiconductor quantum dots* written by Xiaohu Gao, Yuanyuan Cui, Richard M. Levenson, Leland W. K. Chung, and Shuming Nie for FERs and *Scientists target tumors with 'quantum' dots* written by Holly Korschun for GRs. Focus on the vocabulary used for the two different types of readers.

Article 1: FER

The structural design involves encapsulating <u>luminescent</u> QEs with an <u>ABC triblock copolymer</u> and linking this amphiphilic polymer to <u>tumor-targeting ligands</u> and drug-delivery functionalities.

Article 2: GR

Encapsulated in a <u>highly protective polymer coating</u> and attached to a monoclonal antibody that guides them to <u>prostate tumor sites</u> in living mice, the quantum dots are <u>visible</u> using a simple mercury lamp.

The text for the FERs includes the words *luminescent*, *ABC triblock copolymer,* and *tumor-targeting ligands.* The text for the GRs uses the more commonly known words *visible, highly protective polymer coating*, and *prostate tumor sites.*

Exercise 1E: Comparing Vocabulary for General and Field Expert Readers

Analyze these two sentences for FERs and GRs. Use a highlighter to mark the words in the second sentence (written for GRs) that have been substituted for the underlined words in the first sentence (written for FERs).

1. These results raise new possibilities for ultrasensitive and <u>multiplexed imaging</u> of molecular targets <u>in vivo</u>.
2. Emory scientists have for the first time used a new class of luminescent "quantum dot" nanoparticles in living animals to simultaneously target and image cancerous tumors.

Which vocabulary do you understand more easily? ___ Article 1 ___ Article 2

Analyzing Texts

Being able to identify a text's audience, its parts, and its vocabulary is an important skill that will help your own writing improve. In the sample text from the article *In vivo cancer targeting and imaging with semiconductor quantum dots* written for FERs, note how the writers target expert readers by using field-specific vocabulary and an organization specific to the community. Examples are noted.

In vivo cancer targeting and imaging with semiconductor quantum dots

Xiaohu Gao, Yuanyuan Cui, Richard M Levenson, Leland W K Chung & Shuming Nie

Abstract (formal research style of organization):

We describe the development of multifunctional nano-particle probes **(field-specific vocabulary)** based on semiconductor quantum dots (QDs) for cancer targeting and imaging in living animals. The structural design involves encapsulating luminescent QDs with an ABC triblock copolymer and linking this amphiphilic polymer to tumor-targeting ligands **(field-specific vocabulary)** and drug-delivery functionalities. In vivo targeting studies of human prostate cancer growing in nude mice indicate that the QD probes accumulate at tumors both by the enhanced permeability and retention of tumor sites and by antibody binding to cancer-specific cell surface biomarkers. Using both subcutaneous injection of QD-tagged **(field-specific vocabulary)** cancer cells and systemic injection of multifunctional QD probes **(field-specific vocabulary)**, we have achieved sensitive and multicolor fluorescence imaging of cancer cells under in vivo conditions. We have also integrated a whole-body macro-illumination system with wavelength-resolved spectral imaging for efficient background removal and precise delineation of weak spectral signatures. These results raise new possibilities for ultra sensitive and multiplexed imaging of molecular targets in vivo.

Exercise 1F: Analysis of Text for General Readers

Analyze an excerpt from the article *Scientists Target Tumors with 'Quantum Dots'* noting how a text for general readers features the implications and importance of the research findings in the field-specific article. Use a highlighter to mark the **vocabulary** that is easier to understand than in the field-specific sample on page 8 and the **definitions and explanations** given for general readers.

Scientists Target Tumors with 'Quantum Dots'

Holly Korschun

Emory scientists have for the first time used a new class of luminescent "quantum dot" nanoparticles in living animals to simultaneously target and image cancerous tumors. Encapsulated in a highly protective polymer coating and attached to a monoclonal antibody that guides them to prostate tumor sites in living mice, the quantum dots are visible using a simple mercury lamp. The scientists believe the ability to both target and image cells in vivo represents a significant step in the quest to use nanotechnology to target, image and treat cancer, cardiovascular plaques and neurodegenerative disease in humans. The findings appeared in the Aug. 1 edition of *Nature Biotechnology.* The research team was led by Shuming Nie, a nanotechnology expert and professor in the joint Emory/Georgia Tech Coulter Department of Biomedical Engineering and the Winship Cancer Institute, and by Lelund Chung, professor of urology in the School of Medicine and Winship.

Quantum dots are nanometer-sized luminescent semiconductor crystals that have unique chemical and physical properties due to their size and highly compact structure. Quantum dots can be chemically linked (conjugated) to molecules such as antibodies, peptides, proteins or DNA and engineered to detect other molecules, such as those present on the surface of cancer cells.

From Korshun, H. (2004, August 23). *Emory Report*, Vol. 57, No. 1, Emory University, Atlanta, Georgia.

Telling Your Story

You will have the opportunity to write about your developing research—"to tell your story" to both general and field expert readers in your academic career as you apply for travel and research grants through your university and outside funding organizations. Successful students find that targeting a particular audience increases their chances of being awarded a grant. To develop your skills in writing for different readers, you can begin by analyzing award-winning student texts and faculty publications.

Examine the two models by Julianne Chung, a PhD student in math, who wrote about her research area for different readers—a general public and a field-specific audience. She won the Computational Science Graduate Fellowship Annual Essay Contest sponsored by the U.S. Department of Energy and a fellowship to fund her research during her graduate doctoral study. By engaging a general public audience successfully by "telling her research story" effectively, she gained support.

Student Model 1: Engages Field Expert Readers

Julianne presents her research "story"—her ideas and claim—for field expert readers in the introductory section of her honors thesis *Filtering Methods for Image Restoration* (unpublished manuscript). She focuses on a field-specific audience: professors reading her honors thesis. In this text, she primarily shares her knowledge about her research focus. Note how she **situates her research with past and current research** and **uses field-specific vocabulary.**

Filtering Methods for Image Restoration

(uses field-specific vocabulary)

Image restoration is the process of removing blur and noise from degraded images to recover an approximation of the original image. This field of imaging technology is becoming increasingly significant in many scientific applications such as astronomy (1, 2,17), medical imaging (1,8,14,16), military, surveillance (1,16), iris scanning (13), microscopy (9,13), and video communication technologies (1,13) (**situates research**). For example, scientists use long-range telescopes to obtain pictures of distant stars and planets. However, due to the distortion caused by the earth's atmosphere and the random interfering light rays coming from various sources, astronomers receive blurred images.

Similarly, doctors and medical technologist obtain images of human anatomy and physiology from radiological machines such as X-ray, Magnetic Resonance Imaging (MRI) and Single Photon Emission Computed Tomography (SPECT). Because the imaging device is located outside of the patient, the body serves as a distorting medium along with random radiation and can corrupt images. In addition, motion of the patient may cause further blurring in the image. With enhancement techniques, though, noise and blur can be filtered from these images, making them easier for doctors to decipher and analyze. Another emerging application of image restoration in the field of medicine is 3D volumetric tuned-aperture computed tomography (TACT) reconstruction **(field-specific vocabulary)**, in which 2D image restoration is introduced and implemented to reconstruct a 3D object (8).

Surveillance is yet another field heavily influenced by image restoration technologies, one that has severe national security implications. For example, law enforcement and forensic scientists use digital restoration techniques to recover faces and license plates from poor-quality security videotapes. More recently, techniques such as the cubic phase mask **(field-specific vocabulary)** are being used to bring all faces in a crowd into focus, no matter their proximity to the camera (3).

In each of these applications, obtaining clearer images can be accomplished by using computer programs to perform image enhancement techniques. This computational process can be complicated, requiring algorithms to solve tens of thousands and, possibly, millions of mathematical equations. However, an accurate and efficient re-construction can be extremely advantageous to the field.

References

1. Mark R. Banham and Aggelos K. Katsaggelos. "Digital Image Restoration." *IEEE Signal Processing Magazine.* March 1997: pp. 24–41.
2. Richard Berry and James Burnell. *The Handbook of Astronomical Image Processing.* Willmann-Bell Inc., Richmond, VA, 2000.
3. Mario Bertero and Patrizia Boccacci. *Introduction to Inverse Problems in Imaging.* IOP Publishing Ltd., London, 1998.
8. P. Hamler, T. Persons, and R. J. Plemmons. "3D Iterative Restoration of Tomosynthetic Images." *OSA Trends in Optics and Photonies, Integrated Computational Imaging Systems, OSA Technical Digest.* Washington, DC, p. 20.
9. Timothy J. Holmes and Yi-Hwa Liu. "Richardson-Lucy/Maximum Likelihood Image Restoration Algorithm for Fluorescence Microscopy: Further Testing." *Applied Optics.* Vol. 28, No. 22, 1989: pp. 4930–4938.
13. Dana Mackenzie. "Novel Imaging Systems Rely on Focus-Free Optics." *SIAM News.* Vol. 36, No. 6, 2003.
14. *Mathematics and Physics of Emerging Biomedical Imaging.* National Research Council Institute of Medicine, National Academy Press, Washington, DC, 1999.
16. Nhat Nguyen, Peyman Milanfar, and Gene Golub. "Efficient Generalized Cross-Validation with Applications to Parametric Image Restoration and Resolution Enhancement." *IEEE Transactions on Image Processing.* Vol. 10, No. 9, 2001.
17. Martin Schweiger, Adam Gibson, and Simon Arridge. "Computational Aspects of Diffuse Optical Tomography." *IEEE Computing in Science and Engineering.* November/December 2003.
18. Jon Van. "Bringing Fuzzy Field into Focus: Image Help for the Hubble." *Chicago Tribune.* December 15, 1991.

Exercise 1G: Identifying Strategies to Engage General Readers

In Student Model 2, Julianne uses a variety of strategies to interest the general public in her fellowship text published in *COMPOSE, The Department of Energy's Computational Science Graduate Fellowship (DOE CSGF) Annual Essay Contest Journal,* 2006. The purpose of the contest is to encourage better communication to general readers of the value of computational science and engineering to society.

To engage GRs, Julianne uses several strategies:

1. Has a creative and interesting title
2. Humanizes the research for less informed readers
3. Creates a visual to show research
4. Uses non-technical vocabulary

Can you find all four features in Julianne's text? Use a highlighter to mark and label them. The first two paragraphs have been done for you as examples.

Student Model 2: Engages a Public Audience and General Readers

Julianne Chung wrote, *"I am a graduate student in the math department, pursuing a PhD in computational mathematics. My primary research is in image restoration—specifically, medical imaging applications. I really enjoyed writing this essay because it challenged me to think about my research from a different perspective. I learned to be more creative and concise in my explanations so that technical concepts don't seem so daunting."*

Making Blurry Images a Thing of the Past

(has a creative and interesting title)

My family loves to take pictures. We see stars on Christmas Eve, not from the twinkling night sky, but from the hundreds of flashes coming from my mom's and aunt's 35 mm cameras. When asked why they take so many pictures, they always respond, "Just in case some of them don't turn out" **(humanizes the research/non-technical vocabulary)**.

Nowadays, the convenience of digital cameras allows us to immediately see our picture and take another if we are unsatisfied. But what if it costs $5,000 to take one picture? Would you pay another $5,000 if the picture was blurry or contaminated with specks of dust? Instead, I think you would try to fix the image you already have **(humanizes the research)**. With the help of advanced mathematics and high-performance computers, researchers are finding new ways to take the blur out of images.

You may be wondering what kind of picture costs $5,000. One example is a medical image from a device called a PET scan. This particular camera can scan for cancer, detect Alzheimer's disease and diagnose heart disease. But the image will be blurred if the subject fidgets. Performing the scan again is costly, not to mention possibly detrimental to the patient's health. The radiologist, which is just a fancy name for a doctor who interprets medical images, must now face a blurred, degraded image of, say, your heart. She has no hope of a clearer image.

The goal of my research is to take that blurry image and work backwards to *"undo"* the blur. The reconstruction must be done using a computer. As a computational scientist, I work to develop sophisticated algorithms or instructions for the computer. Now, a good detective knows that prior to starting any major operation, we need the proper tools and research. That is, we need some knowledge about our problem. The first line of investigation is determining what caused the blur. There could be many culprits; one example is motion blur. If you take a picture of a fast-moving car, you may see lines and streaks in the image. Many photographers desire this artistic effect, but medical doctors and radiologists want to eliminate it. To alleviate the smearing effects, the radiologist will ask you to lie still during the test. No matter how hard you try, you will breathe, itch, sneeze and/or twitch, thereby causing motion blur in the image.

Once we know the kinds of blur contaminating our image, the next step is to arm ourselves with the tools needed to do the reconstruction. We start with the basics. A digital image is a picture sitting inside a computer. Each image consists of pixels that snap together in a grid-like formation. Each pixel has an associated value, like each tile of a mosaic has its own color. A typical medical image has a grid of 256 pixels by 256 pixels, giving a total of 65,536 pixels in the image. That's equivalent to the seating capacity of a large football stadium. Now imagine we line up all the players and fans into one single-file line and assign each person a number. This is similar to how images are stored in the computer. We organize them by putting all 65,536 pixel values into a very long list, making it easier to access each value individually. Remember that our goal is to "undo" the blur in the image. Thus, it is important to understand what happens during the blur process. We do this through mathematical modeling, which is just a fancy expression for using math to explain real-life phenomena. For example, suppose we want to motion blur. Imagine a scenerio in which we paint red, yellow and blue stripes side-by-side on the wall. While the paint is still wet, a child runs his fingers straight through all the colors. The mixture of paints causes a rainbow of colors to appear. In the same way that the motion of the kid's hand causes the colors to mix along the wall, motion in an image causes an average (or smearing) of neighboring pixel values. Mathematically, this phenomenon is characterized by a formula we learned in elementary school: to compute an average, sum up the values and divide by the total number of items. Since a typical image has 65,536 pixels, we have to do this "averaging" 65,536 times! That's a lot of values to manage, so computational scientists conveniently store the information in a large table. This is where computers are helpful and important. Not only do we have to store all of these numbers, but massive computing power also is required to execute instructions that work with these huge tables. So far, we seem to have everything needed to perform the reconstruction, but we have overlooked the most notorious villain of all: the "specks of dust" on the image, which scientists call noise. Looking at an image degraded by noise is like trying to see an image behind the black and white static in a bad TV transmission. Due to the random or accidental nature of noise, the chance of us ever getting back to the exact original image now is like finding a pin in a haystack the size of China. I and many other researchers are trying to solve this problem. No definitive answer has been found, but we will NOT give up.

Even though we cannot reconstruct the original image, many computational mathematicians and researchers are investigating ways to get a good approximation. With the advent of novel mathematical techniques and the help of modern computer technologies, we are getting closer and closer to finding a reliable and automated way to "undo" the blur in any image. Clearing up blurry images is important to many aspects of life, whether to clear up the motion blur in your $5,000 PET scan or to avoid taking yet another family photograph. With my research, maybe one day I will be able to convince my family that one picture is enough.

From Chung J. (2004), published in *COMPOSE: The DOE Annual Essay Contest Journal,* Krell Institute.

Writing Assignment: Brief Research Interest Statements

Prepare two research interest statements.

1. Write a 200-word statement introducing your research interest to a general reader. Think about your interest from the public's perspective and how you can communicate this to the public. Engage the audience with an opening sentence, state what you know about the subject, why you are interested in the area, and the possible applications of the research. Use the ideas and strategies on page 12 to engage the readers.
2. Write a 200-word statement introducing your research interest to field expert reader (professors who share your research interest). Think about your interest from their perspective. Engage them with an opening sentence, state what you know about the subject, why you are interested in the subject, and the possible applications of the research.

Using Academic Language

As you write, you will want to present your ideas vividly and precisely with formal, academic language focused on your readers—both general and field expert. You will want to consciously build an inventory of general and field-specific academic vocabulary to clearly state and explain your ideas and claims, so the readers will not have to infer or guess your meaning. You will want to avoid vocabulary used in informal conversation. For maximum strategic benefit, do not try to learn hundreds of words at a time. Find ten new verbs and adjectives weekly that best suit your field. You can start by reviewing articles published in your field of study related to your research interest or by your professors. Use a highlighter to mark the verbs and nouns and make sure you know their meaning. Keep a glossary of these words and start to incorporate them into your writing.

By beginning to use two basic techniques, you can show marked improvement in your choice of vocabulary.

1. Select strong action verbs that readers can visualize.
2. Choose meaningful, precise adjectives, adverbs, and nouns.

Using Strong Action Verbs (Vocabulary Technique 1)

Skilled academic writers know that English is full of strong, one-word verbs that carry specific meaning, and they use them to present a straightforward, interesting, and clear text. They substitute common weak verbs and two- or three-word verbs for others that present a visual image of the action. Note these examples before studing the list.

1. Researchers have found out that this drug has serious side effects.
   Researchers have **discovered** *that this drug has serious side effects.*
2. Students are under intense pressure to excel in academia.
   Students **face** *intense pressure to excel in academia.*
3. The best-selling author got a contract to write two more novels.
   The best-selling author **signed** *a contract to write two more novels.*
4. There will be a long and painful process for the improvement of the developing country's economy.
   The developing country's economy **will improve** *after a long and painful process.*

You can begin to build an inventory of strong verbs by substituting common, weak verbs with the most frequently used verbs in all academic disciplines listed. Use a highlighter to mark any verbs that you do not know and learn the meaning.

abandon	advocate	assess	equate	involve
accelerate	affiliate	assume	establish	presume
access	agitate	comply	evaluate	prevail
accompany	aid	conclude	guarantee	proceed
accomplish	align	construct	identify	publish
accumulate	allege	consult	illustrate	pursue
achieve	allude	define	impact	require
adhere	alter	denote	imply	specify
adjust	analyze	derive	indicate	sum
administer	approach	devise	interpret	vary

Adapted from a chart published *Teaching Academic ESL Writing* by Eli Hinkel, Lawrence Erlbaum, 2004.

Exercise 1H: Using Strong Action Verbs

Match the weak verb in the left column with a strong verb in the right column by drawing a line between them.

Set 1

1. give out	alter
2. be in favor of	administer
3. change	approach
4. join	aid
5. stir up; mix up	affiliate
6. help	analyze
7. study	advocate
8. come near; make contact with	assume
9. take for granted; think	agitate

Set 2

1. be different	proceed
2. go; carry on	interpret
3. set up; start	establish
4. see; find	vary
5. need, call for	indicate
6. get someone involved	involve
7. be a sign of; point to	identify
8. figure out	require

Exercise 1I: Identifying Strong Verb Usage

Analyze the two brief research interest statements that you wrote for the Writing Assignment on page 16 for verb usage. Underline all verbs, and replace as many as you can with strong, visual verbs. Refer to the list of academic verbs on page 17. Rewrite your statements.

Exercise 1J: Peer Review of Verb Usage

Ask a classmate to review your research interest statements for verb usage and to give suggestions for additional strong verbs. Follow the feedback by substituting weak verbs in your statements. List the verbs to replace on the left. Write a replacement on the right.

______________________	______________________
______________________	______________________
______________________	______________________
______________________	______________________
______________________	______________________

Avoiding Be *Verbs*

You may be surprised to learn how frequently you use weak *be* verbs. You probably use the empty constructions *there is/are* and *it* and overuse the **passive voice.** This is not to say that you should never use the passive voice, but you should use it appropriately. Since the passive voice includes a form of the verb *be*, you can easily recognize it. Note these examples:

> The experiment <u>was completed</u> in a timely manner.
>
> The orchestra <u>is conducted</u> by a famous musician from Italy.

The sentences focus first on the action and not who performs the action of the verb. If you want to direct your readers' attention to the result of an action, and the "agent" or "actor" is unimportant, then you will want to use the passive voice. Writers in the sciences commonly use the passive voice in lab reports and scientific research papers, particularly in the materials and methods section, when they want to focus attention on the experiment and not necessarily on who performed the experiment.

If you find yourself using the passive voice often, you can change your sentences into the active voice by using strong, active verbs. First, identify which noun is actually performing the action and move it to the beginning of the sentence to function as the subject. Second, place the new, strong verb you selected to replace the weak *be* verb and place it after the subject. Then rewrite the rest of the sentence. For example:

> Interesting results were found by the research group.
>
> *The research group* **discovered** *interesting results.*

Notice how the research group, the "actor" of the verb becomes the subject at the beginning and the stronger verb, *discovered* follows the subject and replaces the weaker verb *were found.*

You can replace many of the *be* verbs in your texts by using these techniques:

1. Use synonyms that can give the same meaning as *to be.*
   - *exist, live, prevail, obtain, seem, appear, look*
   - *occur, happen*
   - *remain, stay, last, continue, endure, survive, persist*
   - *attend, follow, accompany*

   > The librarian is at the library until 8 PM.
   >
   > The librarian **remains** at the library until 8 PM.

2. Use simple verb forms (progressive -ing forms are rare in academic writing).

   > Witchcraft was altering social behavior by using spells, charms, and potions.
   >
   > Witchcraft **altered** social behavior by using spells, charms, and potions.

3. Use active voice when possible (passive focuses on what is done rather than who does it).

   > The women were prosecuted for sorcery and witchcraft.
   >
   > The colonial viceroyalty **prosecuted** the women for sorcery and witchcraft.

Exercise 1K: Reducing the Number of *Be* Verbs

Do a search to determine how many forms of *be* you used in the research interest statements. Circle all *be* forms, and substitute them with strong verbs.

List the *be* verbs you used on the left. Write a replacement on the right.

Exercise 1L: More Practice Reducing the Number of *Be* Verbs

Rewrite the sentences by replacing the underlined *be* forms.

1. This means that every organ and every cell are the same age and are working as a single unit.

2. Medical research is using genetic engineering to improve health treatment.

3. These questions are acute for each and every one of us.

4. Mitchelet's research was adding to studies conducted in the sixteenth century.

Using Precise Adjectives, Adverbs, and Nouns (Vocabulary Technique 2)

The second technique to improve your language use is to select precise adjectives, adverbs, and nouns. Many words—especially spoken vocabulary—can be interpreted differently and convey little or no meaning. If you write the way you speak, you will use too many vague and informal words. Note how the sentences containing vague adjectives, adverbs, and nouns have been rewritten to be more formal and concise or with vocabulary expressing clear and exact meaning.

> The government has made good progress in solving some environmental problems.
>
> > The government **has made** progress in solving environmental problems.
>
> The results of a lot of different (vague and informal) projects have been pretty good (vague).
>
> > The results of **ten projects** have been **accepted.**
>
> A loss of jobs is one of the things that will happen if the process is automated.
>
> > A loss of jobs is one of the **consequences** if the process is automated.

The informal, vague adjectives and nouns listed are used frequently in conversation; however, you should avoid them in writing since they do not convey exactness in meaning to your readers. Consult a **thesaurus** (a book containing synonyms for words) for substitutions.

a few	an	considerable	interesting	really more
a great deal	awful	enough	kind of	much
about	bad	excellent	large	relatively
adequate	better	good	less	significant
a lot of	big	great	many	some
amazing	brilliant	hardly	pretty	sort of

Exercise 1M: *Using Academic Vocabulary*

Substitute the underlined nouns, verbs, adjectives, and adverbs with more formal language. Some sentences may require a change in structure.

1. Building a nuclear power plant will not get rid of the energy problem completely.
2. The researchers got encouraging results.
3. The molecular process that turns good cells into malignant ones is unclear.
4. There are a number of diseases caused by genetic disorders.
5. The International Geochemical Mapping Project is an excellent example of the collaboration of international chemists.
6. In a recent TV program about tampering with nature, the question of whether genetic engineering and human cloning are good or bad was raised.
7. A long period of time is needed for people to accept the new concept and recognize the benefit.
8. Progress in human life is the aim of science and technology.
9. Genetic engineering is a helpful tool that moves forward the development.

Exercise 1N: Using Strong Verbs

Edit the paragraph by the U.S. Geological Survey to substitute active verbs for the underlined passive forms. Some sentences may need to be combined or changed in structure.

USGS Unveils How Earthquakes Pose Risks to Afghanistan

While human-induced rumblings have dominated life in Afghanistan for several decades, a more natural hazard may present a significant threat to this country undergoing massive restoration: earthquakes. The Islamic Republic of Afghanistan is located in a geologically active part of the world. Each year, Afghanistan is struck by moderate to strong earthquakes, and every few years, a powerful earthquake causes significant damage or fatalities. The seriousness of this hazard was poignantly demonstrated by the magnitude 7.6 earthquake on October 8, 2005, in nearby Kashmir, Pakistan, that caused more than 80,000 fatalities and left an estimated four million people homeless. Without planning for the potential devastation that earthquakes can wreak, years of investment in restoration of Afghanistan infrastructure could be undermined in a matter of seconds.

Exercise 1O: Peer Review Language Use

Ask a classmate to evaluate your research interest statements for language use by highlighting the vague adjectives, adverbs, and nouns. Replace the highlighted words to make your writing stronger. List three words you fixed as a result.

____

____

____

UNIT **2**

Paragraphs: The Building Blocks of Writing

"I would argue that the paragraph, not the sentence, is the basic unit of writing—the place where coherence begins and words stand a chance of becoming more than mere words . . . Topic sentence followed by support and description insists that the writer organize his/her thoughts, and it also provides good insurance from wandering away from the topic."

—Stephen King, novelist

Writers build meaning in extended texts with words, sentences, and paragraphs. The order of words in sentences in English determines the meaning of a single thought, and the order of sentences in paragraphs constructs the meaning of one general theme or thought with multiple levels of examples and details. To develop a long piece of writing, writers use paragraphing to guide readers through a central claim supported with various main ideas or points and levels of detail for each idea. If your writing is hard to read because the information does not contain focused paragraphs that organize the details of your claim, readers may become confused, lose interest, and not finish reading your writing. English readers expect the paragraphs to move your central claim through the whole piece with illustrative and concrete details and a clear pattern of organization.

You will need to construct each paragraph carefully based on your purpose and readers, selecting from a variety of patterns of organizations: general to specific, process, comparative, problem-solution, and cause and effect. This unit focuses on the **general to specific paragraph arrangement**, a core pattern in English writing in which the general topic is first and details become more specific as the paragraph continues. You will frequently find it in academic essays, the introduction sections of research papers, opening paragraphs in discussions and analyses, biographical statements, research briefs, and essay exam questions—to name a few. You will learn to build **clear paragraph units** in a biographical statement, a common and important text that presents events in your life. By creating a **biographical statement** that includes interesting details and is adaptable for multiple readers throughout your studies and career, you can display your experience and attributes.

One-Paragraph Components

> "Details make the difference between boring and terrific writing. It's the difference between a pencil sketch and a lush oil painting. As a writer, words are your paint. Use all color."
>
> —Rhys Alexander in *Writing Gooder*

When using the general to specific paragraph arrangement you should include three components of information: a general statement or topic sentence, primary support sentences, and secondary support sentences. The general statement or topic sentence immediately creates a familiar map in the mind of the readers—general to specific information. The readers know the theme of your paragraph and expect to find concrete and understandable details to help them comprehend and visualize this general theme. Your choice of details will determine the picture you paint for the readers. Try to picture the structure of a paragraph as a top to bottom structure with different levels of generality about a theme or an assertion. Imagine a pyramid or triangle with the point at the bottom. The top level begins with the topic sentence followed by multiple levels of details and examples referred to as primary and secondary support. The primary support is more detailed and would be the middle section of the triangle or pyramid. The secondary support is even more specific and is the narrowest point of the pyramid. These primary and secondary levels of support illustrate concretely and provide credibility for the topic. The **paragraph structure chart** (Figure 2, see page 27) can help you visualize this top to bottom structure.

Figure 2: Paragraph Structure Chart

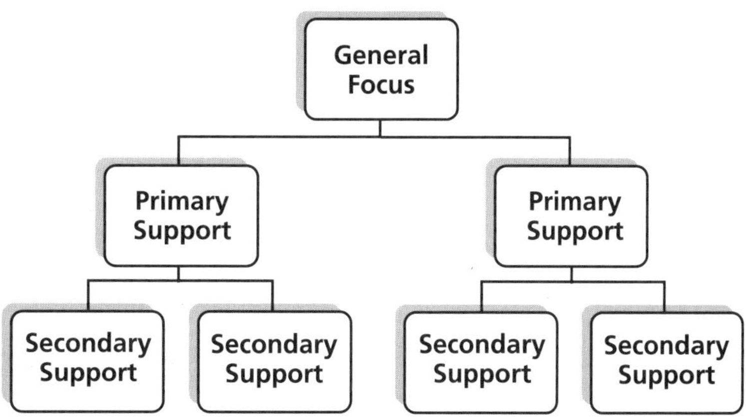

Determining the number of primary and secondary ideas in an academic paragraph is not always easy, so applying the general rule of having two to three primary ideas and at least two secondary ideas for each primary idea in a paragraph can be helpful. Read the paragraph about science (Turkle, *Falling for Science,* 2009) illustrating a general topic sentence and details that visualize the theme for the readers.

> Science is fueled by passion, a passion that often attaches to the world of objects much as the artist attaches to his paints, the poet to his or her words. Putting children in a rich object world is essential to giving science a chance. Children will make intimate connections, connections they need to construct on their own. At a time when science education is in crisis, giving science its best chance means guiding children to objects they can love.

Exercise 2A: Recognizing Top-to-Bottom Structure

Read the paragraph about good thinkers from Stephen D. Krashen's book *Explorations in Language Acquisition and Use* (Heinemann, 2003). Notice the top-to-bottom structure, and answer the questions.

① Studies of "good thinkers" also give us some reason to believe that reading makes you smarter. ② Good thinkers, however they are defined, read a great deal and have read a great deal. ③ Simonton (1988) concluded that "omnivorous reading in childhood and adolescence correlates positively with ultimate adult success." ④ Schaefer and Anastasi (1968) reported that high school students considered to be creative read more than average students, with more creative students reporting that they read over fifty books per year. ⑤ Emery and Csikszentmihalyi (1982) compared fifteen men of very similar background who became college professors with fifteen men of very similar background who grew up to become blue-collar workers. ⑥ The future professors lived in a much more print-rich environment and did far more reading when they were young.

References

Emery, C., and M. Csikszentmihalyi. 1982. "The socialization effects of cultural role models in otogenetic development and upward mobility." *Child Psychiatry and Human Development,* 12: 3–19.

Schaefer, C.E., Anastasi, A. 1968. "A biographical inventory for identifying creativity in adolescent boys." *Journal of Applied Psychology*, 52: 42–48.

Simonton, D.K. 1988. *Scientific genius: A psychology of science.* Cambridge, UK: Cambridge University Press.

1. What is the general focus (or top level) of the paragraph? ____________________
   ____
2. What is the primary support idea? ____________________
   ____
3. How many secondary support ideas are included? ____________________
4. Which sentences show the secondary support? ____________________
   ____

Exercise 2B: *Analysis of Paragraph Structure*

A famous speech by John F. Kennedy on space exploration illustrates how the general focus of the paragraph (the topic sentence) guides the reader through the paragraph with brilliant detail. Read an excerpt from the speech, and use a highlighter to mark the detail that illustrates each **bolded** time span.

John F. Kennedy's Moon Speech—Rice Stadium/September 12, 1962

No man can fully grasp how far and how fast we have come, but condense, if you will, the **50,000 years** of man's recorded history in a time span of but a half-century. Stated in these terms, we know very little about the **first 40 years**, except at the end of them advanced man had learned to use the skins of animals to cover them. Then about **10 years ago**, under this standard, man emerged from his caves to construct other kinds of shelter. Only **five years ago** man learned to write and use a cart with wheels. Christianity began less than two years ago. The printing press came **this year**, and then less than **two months ago**, during this whole 50-year span of human history, the steam engine provided a new source of power. Newton explored the meaning of gravity. **Last month** electric lights and telephones and automobiles and airplanes became available. Only **last week** did we develop penicillin and television and nuclear power, and **now** if America's new spacecraft succeeds in reaching Venus, we will have literally reached the stars before midnight tonight. This is a breathtaking pace, and such a pace cannot help but create new ills as it dispels old, new ignorance, new problems, new dangers. Surely the opening vistas of space promise high costs and hardships, as well as high reward.

From *Key Documents in the History of Space Policy.* National Aeronautics and Space Administration.

Biographical Statements

Even though the purpose of paragraphs vary, the components remain the same. For example, you will frequently create a common academic text, a biographical statement, to present yourself as a credible member of a community. These paragraphs should contain an organized structure with the three components of information. Note the outline for a biographical statement written by a math professor illustrates the components in the proper order: a topic sentence, three primary support ideas, and secondary support ideas.

Dr. James Nagy has specialized in mathematics during his extensive career. (Topic Sentence)

→ *Education* **(Primary Support)**

He was awarded a BS in Mathematics in 1986 and an MS in Computational Mathematics in 1998, both from Northern Illinois University.

In 1991, he was awarded a PhD in Applied Mathematics from North Carolina State University.

→ *Work Experience* **(Primary Support)**

He was a Postdoctoral Research Associate at the Institute of Mathematics and its Applications, University of Minnesota, from 1991–1992, and a member of the faculty in the Department of Mathematics at Southern Methodist University, Dallas, from 1992–1999.

Since 1999 he has been a member of the faculty in the Mathematics and Computer Science Department at Emory University in Atlanta, Georgia.

Work Experience Detail **(Secondary Support)**

In 2001, he was selected to hold the Emory Professorship for Distinguished Teaching in the Social and Natural Sciences.

→ *Publications* **(Primary Support)**

He has published many research papers on scientific computing, numerical linear algebra, inverse problems, and image processing.

Publication Detail (Secondary Support)

His particular research interests are in the numerical solution of large-scale structured linear systems.

Now read the same biographical statement written in paragraph form and visualize the components from the outline.

> Dr. James Nagy has specialized in mathematics during his extensive career. He was awarded a BS in Mathematics in 1986 and an MS in Computational Mathematics in 1998 both from Northern Illinois University. In 1991, he was awarded a PhD in Applied Mathematics from North Carolina State University. He was a Postdoctoral Research Associate at the Institute of Mathematics and its Applications, University of Minnesota, from 1991–1992, and a member of the faculty in the Department of Mathematics at Southern Methodist University, Dallas, from 1992–1999. Since 1999 he has been a member of the faculty in the Mathematics and Computer Science Department at Emory University, Atlanta. In 2001, he was selected to hold the Emory Professorship for Distinguished Teaching in the Social and Natural Sciences. He has published many research papers on scientific computing, numerical linear algebra, inverse problems, and image processing. His particular research interests are in the numerical solution of large scale structured linear systems.

Exercise 2C: *Analyzing Biographical Statements*

Read the biographical statement, and identify the general focus of each paragraph.

Daniel Domingues, a student in the History Department at Emory University, studies Atlantic history and Modern Age slavery. He specializes in Brazil's trans-Atlantic slave trade and the commerce of captives in the western coast of Africa.

Back ground

Before studying at Emory, Daniel completed a bachelor's degree in history at the Federal University of Rio de Janeiro, Brazil, in 2004 with an honor's thesis on the western islands' slave trade of Africa. This research was supported by grants from the National Council for Technological and Scientific Development and the Foundation for Research Support of the State of Rio de Janeiro. Daniel's interest in historical documentation led him to work for the Brazilian Archeology Institute, where he developed research projects on colonial history of that country with a special focus on the world of the captives.

Academic history

Daniel continues his research focusing on the impact of slave trade on African societies. During the summer of 2005, he traveled to Angola through a grant received from the Institute of National Archives/Tombo Tower and the Luso-American Foundation for Development in Portugal. He also traveled to Portugal during the summer of 2006 to further this research. Currently, he is contributing to a research project entitled "Voyages: the Trans-Atlantic Slave Trade Database" that will track every slaving voyage that sailed across the Atlantic Ocean during the Modern Age.

experienced
current interest

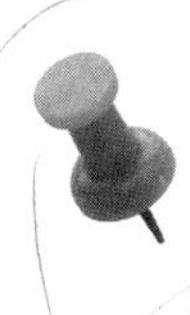

Writing Assignment: Brief Biographical Statement

Write a biographical statement to post on a website, in a department newsletter, or for a publication. The purpose of this writing is to showcase your academic qualities, past experiences, and research interests and to present yourself as a competent member of the community. To avoid "wandering" from your topic, follow these steps:

1. Outline your ideas using the components of a typical general to specific paragraph arrangement.
2. Write one paragraph. Include five sentences (topic, three primary ideas, and a final statement). The three primary sentences can include your education, work experience, and research interests.
3. Write the paragraph again, and expand it to 10–11 sentences. You should insert two secondary support ideas to illustrate each of the three primary ideas.

From Paragraph to Whole Text

Some biographical statements are powerful because they focus on a unique theme carried though multiple paragraphs and humanize the writer. The **theme chart** (Figure 3) can help you visualize how a theme can be used throughout the statement. By carrying a theme in the first paragraph throughout the whole text, you will draw the readers' attention to an important central idea about you which might be critical to your receiving a fellowship, internship, or publication acceptance. If you write the same chronological statement for applications, presentations, proposals, funding, and professional positions in this competitive, academic, and professional environment, you will fail to capture the readers' attention. Analyze the two biographical statements written by the same person.

Figure 3: Theme Chart

Theme	
Areas of Specialization and Interest	• Past • Current
Education	• University Level • Specialized Training
Publications	• Past • Current Interest

Student Model 1: Maintains a Central Focus

Notice how each paragraph in Student Model 1 has a central focus. Paragraph 1 focuses on educational background, Paragraph 2 on research interests, and Paragraph 3 on her career as a writer.

Margarita Pintado, a graduate student in the Spanish Department at Emory University, studied Journalism and Mass Media Communications at the University of Puerto Rico from August 1999 to May 2003. During that time, she collaborated on magazine, newspaper, "cyber-journalism," and firm projects. After completing her Bachelor's degree, she entered the Graduate Department of Hispanic Studies at the same institution. Before finishing her Master's degree, she moved to Atlanta to initiate a PhD degree in Spanish.

Her current studies focus on Contemporary Latino American and Caribbean Literature. Her writing reveals a strong concern with the new and different literary styles that describe those countries. She explores the impact of post modernism on such authors as Pedro Juan Gutiérrez, Fernando Vallejo, Leonardo Padura, Rita Indiana Hernández, and others. One of her most significant research areas illustrates the step between magical realism to dirty realism, or in other words, the transition from illusion and hope to disappointment and pessimism. Several of her investigative essays have been published in academic magazines such as Revista de Estudios Hispánicos, Letras, Derivas and Claridad.

Besides her interests in Literature, Margarita has started a career as a writer. Last year she published the short story "Negativos de arena," from *The Anthology Cuentos de Oficio* (Terranova Editors, 2005), a compilation of new literary voices. Currently, she publishes articles for different literary magazines in the United States.

Student Model 2: Carries a Unique Theme Throughout

Note how the writer includes a unique theme in Student Model 2 (underlining) and carries the theme through each paragraph. The writer has focused this biographical statement to readers interested in her interdisciplinary interests.

Margarita Pintado focuses her research in projects related to journalism and social issues. Currently, in a PhD program in Hispanic literature, she has discovered a new interdisciplinary perspective with writing which bridges her interests in literature and society.

Born in Puerto Rico, Ms. Pintado always loved writing and literature as a child. Evidence of literature was always present in her home, where the solicited toys were books. As a high school and college student, Ms. Pintado discovered journalism that focused her concerns on the social aspects of justice, freedom, equality, and diversity. Through journalism, her interests as a writer and as conscious citizen connected.

After she finished her Bachelor's degree in Journalism at La Universidad de Puerto Rico, Recinto de Río Piedras, she moved to Atlanta to enroll in a PhD program in Hispanic Literature at Emory University continuing her research interests related to Hispanic literature and social issues. Ms. Pintado has started a career as a writer and has recently published a short story "Negativos de arena" in *The Anthology Cuentos de Oficio* (Terranova editors, 2005), a compilation of new literary voices.

Exercise 2D: More Analyzing Biographical Statements

Answer these questions about the models. Then talk about your answers in a group.

1. Which model do you prefer? Why? ____

   ____

2. Where do you think Margarita will use Model 1? __________________________________

   ____

3. Where might Margarita use Model 2? ____

   ____

Writing Assignment: Biographical Statement

Draft a biographical statement of 250–300 words (with at least three paragraphs) to situate you within your department or a particular field or profession. Consider the statement as part of an application packet for a travel grant to advance your research in another country. This statement should identify your current position, major accomplishments, interests, and concerns. Select a unique theme for the biographical statement, and make sure you carry the theme throughout the statement. Take notes using the outline on page 37 before starting to draft the statement.

Outline

Audience: ______________________________

Faculty?

Administrators?

Students?

Other?

Purpose/Theme: ______________________________

Central Focus?

Unique Theme?

Organization: ______________________________

Each paragraph has a focus that connects to the theme?

General to specific?

Primary Support: ______________________________

____

____

Academic background?

Current position?

Past positions?

Research interests?

General interests?

Publications?

Awards?

Honors?

Secondary Support: ______________________________

____

Details?

Examples?

Rewrite as a Critical Thinker

Skilled writers know that the first draft is never the only or final draft. As you evaluate and rewrite your ideas, you will discover more details and often reframe your thoughts. Think of rewriting not as a chore but as an opportunity to create your claims and ideas visually with multiple levels of detail for a specific audience. You will learn how to revise in detail in Units 6 and 7, but for now you can begin the process of rewriting by focusing on the areas studied in Units 1 and 2.

Exercise 2E: Revising

Revise the first draft of your biographical statement after putting it aside for a few hours or a day. Read it again, evaluating it for audience.

1. Are your readers general readers or field expert readers?

____

____

2. How much do the readers know about you?

____

____

3. How interested are the readers in your biographical statement?

____

____

4. How can you make the readers interested?

____

____

Based on your answers, add, delete, or move ideas, and then rewrite your statement. At this point, don't worry about grammar; individual issues will be addressed in Unit 7. Read the steps, and check them as you complete them.

Steps	Completed
1. Read the text without stopping.	
2. Insert ideas for additional content or cross out content for deletion.	
3. Highlight the central theme or focus in the first, introductory paragraph.	
4. Underline or draw lines connecting words and phrases in the second, third, and fourth supporting paragraphs that link to the theme.	
5. Highlight the central topic (or main idea) in each paragraph.	
6. Number the multi-level support sentences in each paragraph.	
7. Insert additional support, if needed.	
8. Rewrite on a separate sheet of paper.	

Using a Rubric to Assess Writing

Your instructor will grade your final draft using the biographical statement grading rubric (page 180). The rubric illustrates the importance of theme, support, and organization. Read the rubric, and ask your instructor to explain any parts that you do not understand. Complete the rubric to assess your final draft of the biographical statement. Compare your analysis to your instructor's.

UNIT 3

Mapping the Flow of Information

"Those who write clearly have readers. Those who write obscurely have commentators."

— Albert Camus,
author, philosopher,
Nobel Prize winner

Readers often complain that a novice writer's ideas do not flow or move cohesively within the paragraphs of a text. Since information in your native language might move differently from English, you might not understand what flow of information means for an English-speaking reader. Flow represents the logical sequence of ideas that creates the big concept in the paragraph. Sentences flow into paragraphs. Paragraphs, in turn, flow into the whole text. You learned in Unit 2 that English readers expect the information in paragraphs to follow a predictable pattern or organization. You also learned one important key to creating logical flow in general to specific paragraphs—connecting the parts with topic sentences and primary and secondary supporting ideas. Unit 3 focuses on additional devices, such as **cohesive devices**, to sequence or map your ideas logically, so the reader sees your text as flowing clearly as it paints the big picture or main concept. You will learn to **connect sentences** as chains of information—each piece linked to the previous one—to **maintain the flow of information** in the paragraph as one unit in a cohesive style, and you will rewrite your biographical statement to improve paragraph unity.

Cohesive Devices

To maintain links between supporting ideas and information in paragraphs, writers use cohesive devices. Cohesive devices are words, phrases, or techniques that connect ideas. You might think of these devices as anchors that hold the ideas together. Strategies include:

1. connecting each sentence in the paragraph to the topic sentence (as learned in Unit 2)
2. using transition words between sentences
3. repeating key words and phrases, or information from sentence to sentence
4. establishing a logical progression of ideas by placing previously mentioned or known information before new information

Topic Sentences

Begin each paragraph with a theme or topic. By doing so, you create a map for your readers. As each idea is anchored to that theme or topic, readers can stay connected to the flow of information because they identify the main focus and expect everything in the paragraph to be a supporting example or detail to support that focus.

Exercise 3A: Analyzing Topic Sentences

Read the paragraph from the National Institutes of Health.

> All clinical trials have guidelines about who can participate. Using inclusion/exclusion criteria is an important principle of medical research that helps to produce reliable results. The factors that allow someone to participate in a clinical trial are called "inclusion criteria" and those that disallow someone from participating are called "exclusion criteria." These criteria are based on such factors as age, gender, the type and stage of a disease, previous treatment history, and other medical conditions. Before joining a clinical trial, a participant must qualify for the study. Some research studies seek participants with illnesses or conditions to be studied in the clinical trial, while others need healthy participants. It is important to note that inclusion and exclusion criteria are not used to reject people personally. Instead, the criteria are used to identify appropriate participants and keep them safe. The criteria help ensure that researchers will be able to answer the questions they plan to study.
>
> From www.clinicaltrials.gov/ct2/info/understand#Q02.

Now answer the questions.

1. What is the theme? Clinical Trial Criteria use
2. Do you find any sentences in the paragraph that do not connect to the theme? ______. If so, which ones? ______

Transition Words

Transition words and phrases signal movement of ideas within paragraphs. They transfer your claim or view forward, and they refer the readers back to a previous idea. With transition words or phrases, you can show the readers that you have connected sentences or paragraphs together and developed a relationship between them. When a sentence begins with transition words, you should place a comma after the word(s). For example:

> *In fact*, green chemistry may provide the best solution to the world's energy problem.

Common relationships and the transition words used to express them are shown.

Relationships	Transition Words
adding information	*additionally, also, moreover, furthermore, similarly, in fact*
introducing an example	*for instance, in this case, to illustrate, to demonstrate, for example*
introduced an additional idea	*in addition, additionally, also, moreover, besides, further, another*
contrasting ideas	*in contrast, on the other hand, however, instead, as a consequence, nonetheless, instead, in spite of*
comparing ideas	*similarly, whereas, while, likewise, by comparison*
summarizing	*in summary, briefly, in short, in conclusion, finally, therefore, hence, on the whole, as a result, to conclude*
showing a sequence of time	*first, next, finally, meanwhile, previously, subsequently, at this point, simultaneously, concurrently, before, after*
showing a sequence of logic	*above all, in conclusion*
expressing an opinion or to emphasized	*unfortunately, undoubtedly, certainly, most importantly, above all*
showing a result or effect	*therefore, consequently, as a result*

Exercise 3B: Inserting Transition Words

Transition words have been removed from this paragraph, which makes the meaning unclear for readers. Insert four transitions (*mainly, for example, in fact,* and *in brief*) to connect the ideas more clearly.

Study Abroad Students as Global Citizens

Oksana Gomas, Study Abroad Advisor

Students who leave their secluded worlds to experience a different environment abroad will gain experience and first-hand knowledge of foreign cultures to help them in a global work environment. They will develop an important asset of patience and understanding of cultural difference. Students who study abroad are often stunned and frustrated to find that they cannot manage simple tasks in a foreign culture with strangers who speak a different language and have different customs. They cannot even call a cab or order a pizza. To manage successfully, they must patiently rely on foreigners to function in a new way. As they grapple with these first-hand experiences in a foreign culture, they will learn about the values, perceptions, and behavior of other nationalities that will prepare them for future positions in businesses and corporations with a diverse work environment.

Exercise 3C: Improving Flow

Read the biographical statement you wrote in Unit 2 (page 36) and check transitions in each paragraph. Can you improve the flow of each paragraph by adding transition words? Make a list of transition words to add. Then rewrite your biographical statement.

____

____

____

____

____

Repetition

Skilled writers also connect ideas within paragraphs by using repetition of key words, synonyms, and pronouns. Note the numerous times the author repeats the key word, *science,* to maintain the flow of ideas for the readers. Also note the underlined nouns with pronouns.

> ① **Science** is fueled by passion, a passion that often attaches to the world of objects much as the *artist* attaches to his paints, the *poet* to his or her words. Putting children in a rich object world is essential to giving
>
> ② **science** a chance. *Children* will make intimate connections, connections they need to construct on their own. At a time when ③ **science** education is in crisis, giving ④ ***science*** its best chance means guiding *children* to objects they can love.
>
> From Turkle, *Falling for Science,* 2009.

Exercise 3D: Recognizing Repetition

Reread the science paragraph. Then use a highlighter to indicate the exact or synonymous repetitions for the listed words. Write the number of the word above each of its repetitions. The first sentence has been done for you as an example.

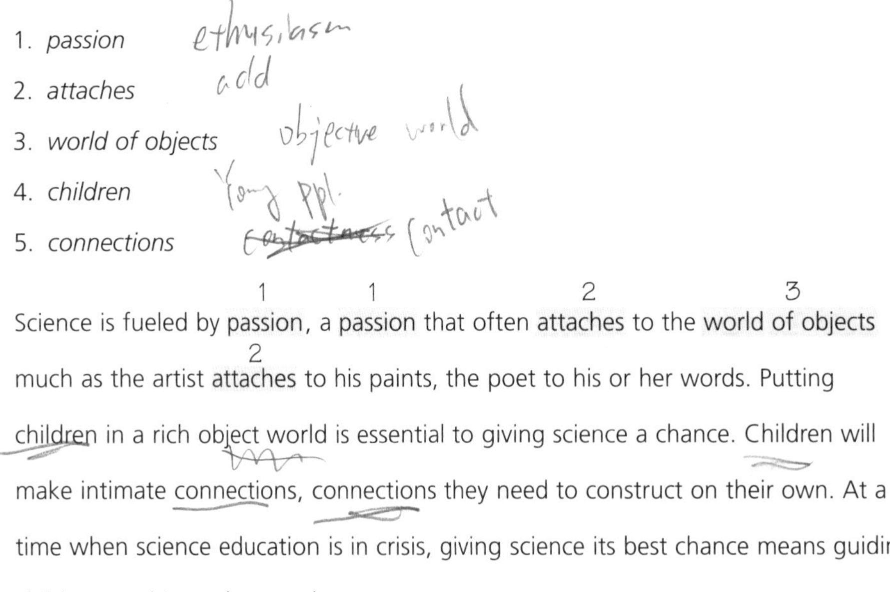

1. *passion*
2. *attaches*
3. *world of objects*
4. *children*
5. *connections*

(1 above "passion", 1 above "passion", 2 above "attaches", 3 above "world of objects")
Science is fueled by passion, a passion that often attaches to the world of objects

(2 above "attaches")
much as the artist attaches to his paints, the poet to his or her words. Putting children in a rich object world is essential to giving science a chance. Children will make intimate connections, connections they need to construct on their own. At a time when science education is in crisis, giving science its best chance means guiding children to objects they can love.

Exercise 3E: Recognizing Repetition

Use a highlighter to mark and number the key words that have exact or synonymous repetition in the paragraph. Underline the repetition.

The Use of Human Stem Cells for Research in Human Diseases

Anthony Luyai, biochemistry PhD student

In general, scientists believe that human embryonic stem cell research holds the hidden keys for management and treatment of many medical conditions that have troubled mankind. These researchers search continuously to acquire knowledge about stem cells and transform the knowledge into tangible products for use as therapeutics for these illnesses. In fact, doctors, patients, and manufacturers eagerly seek stem cell products for maladies with no current cure. However, many people question this rush to engineer and develop these expensive body spare parts because they believe that only the rich will benefit, and the manufacturers will reap outlandish profits from these expensive parts.

Exercise 3F: Revising

Analyze your biographical statement for repetition. Mark the exact or synonymous repetitions, and insert new ones if needed.

Previously Mentioned versus New Information

Writers place known—*commonly understood*—or previously mentioned information—*already presented*—at the beginning of sentences and new information at the end of sentences. Note how the new information in one sentence is expanded in the next sentence.

During World War II, women in western countries participated very actively in the war effort (**common knowledge**) and quickly became the cornerstone of the economy (**new information**). The growing power of women as wage earners (**previously mentioned information**) began to challenge the old patriarchal order that had prevailed (**new information**).

Exercise 3G: Previously Mentioned versus New Information

Read the paragraphs, and mark the previously mentioned and new information in each sentence. Use a highlighter to mark the new information, and underline the previously mentioned or known information.

HIV Drug Resistance: Current Threats

Duc Bui Nguyen, graduate student in clinical research

Since the human immunodeficiency virus (HIV) was discovered, it quickly became the leading cause of morbidity and mortality around the world. In the battle against this deadly virus, many anti-HIV drugs, called antiretrovirals or ARVs, have been developed and used in patients. However, patients soon showed evidence of resistance to the drug. This resistance is now one of the biggest concerns of scientists and doctors worldwide. Even though apprehension about the problem exists, a thorough assessment has not been performed. Without a comprehensive and meticulous assessment, the battle to stop AIDS may be lost.

Unlocking Mysteries of the Parthenon

The Parthenon was part of an ambitious building campaign on the Acropolis that began around 450 BC. A generation before, the Athenians, as part of an alliance of Greek city-states, had led heroic victories against Persian invaders. This alliance would evolve into a *de facto* empire under Athenian rule, and some 150 to 200 cities across the Aegean began paying Athens huge sums of what amounted to protection money. Basking in glory, the Athenians planned their new temple complex on a lavish, unprecedented scale—with the Parthenon as the centerpiece. Surviving fragments of the financial accounts, which were inscribed in stone for public scrutiny, have prompted estimates of the construction budget that range from around 340 to 800 silver talents—a considerable sum in an age when a single talent could pay a month's wages for 170 oarsmen on a Greek warship.

From Hadingham, E. "Efforts to restore the ancient temple of Athena are yielding new insights." *Smithsonian* (February 2008). www.smithsonianmag.com/.

Writing Assignment: Rewriting for Paragraph Unity (Flow of Information)

Read the biographical statement and the research interest statement that you wrote (page 36). Make sure that the information flows well. Read the checklist of items needed, and check them as you complete them.

Items	Completed
1. Support sentences connected to the topic sentence	
2. Transition words	
3. Repetition	
4. Substitution	
5. Previously mentioned information	
6. New information	

Ask a classmate to review your revised draft and to mark each of these items in the text. Follow the advice by making any necessary changes, additions, or deletions. Rewrite your statement and narrative on a separate piece of paper.

UNIT 4

Reader Expectations

"Readers, after all, are making the world with you. You give them the materials, but it's the readers who build that world in their minds."

—Ursula K. Le Guin, author

The challenges you face as an academic writer may seem daunting to you with the demand to write lengthy, multi-paragraph texts for distinct audiences. You may wonder how you can possibly master writing quickly enough to succeed in your academic assignments. You cannot become an expert and skilled writer in a few weeks, but you can start to think about writing as your readers do. You learned an essential feature expected by readers in Unit 3: clear flow of information within paragraphs. This unit will introduce three additional features that readers expect: a **unique perspective or claim, macro structure**, and **credible support.** By providing your readers with these features, you can make sure they pay attention to your ideas, and you will see immediate improvement and clarity in your writing. Whether you write a research paper, lab report, summary, interpretation of poems and novels, case studies, or essays, you will find these qualities essential. Of course, you will have to learn specific conventions and standards expected in your field of study, but these three features reflect the core of academic texts. This unit will help you use these features and create a claim or thesis statement for general readers that you can incorporate into a research interest essay in Unit 6.

Unique Perspective or Claim

"Why do writers write? Because it isn't there."

—Thomas Berger, novelist

Academic scholars engage in discussions about new developments, information, and facts by analyzing, defending, refuting, and offering new views and questions, and they write about these ideas. Your professors expect you to participate in this scholarly conversation by raising research questions or responses that express your unique thoughts and contribute to your field and research. For your writing to impact your field of study, you should do more than state facts; you should always listen to and respond to the dialogue among scholars—to what "they say" as Gerald Graff and Cathy Birkenstein suggest in their book *They Say/I Say—the Moves That Matter in Academic Writing* (W.W. Norton and Company, Inc., 2006). You will find a unique perspective or claim as you participate in these conversations. To write skillfully, place your unique perspective or claim early in the text, and include these three components in the resulting thesis statement, so the readers will know what to expect:

- **what** your claim is about
- **how** you plan to prove the claim
- **why** the claim is significant

To create a topic or research area that interests you, start by raising a question that needs to be answered or that you want to research. This question will be the thread that you carry throughout your writing. Analyze the questions raised by former students, and notice how they turned them into a thesis statement or claim and included the main support ideas.

1. How did African slavery occur in the United States?

   <u>Thesis Statement</u>: The transition from indigenous and European labor to African slavery in the U.S. (What?) resulted primarily from economic, demographic, and cultural reasons (How?) causing the concept of freedom to be non-existent (Why?).

2. How can the convergence (search of the most approximate value of X) of the CGS method be improved?

   Thesis Statement: By analyzing the cause of divergence in the convergent process and the approach of modification of algorithms (How?), the convergence (search of the most approximate value of X) of the CGS method (What?) will be greatly improved so that calculations for industries will be much more convenient (Why?).

3. Why should doctors focus on biological factors when predicting disease risks?

   Thesis Statement: Contrasting the prediction reliability of biological factors versus nurturing factors in three case studies (How?) will show why doctors should first focus on biology when predicting disease risks (What?) for improved diagnostic accuracy (Why?).

Exercise 4A: Identifying Main Points in a Thesis Statement

Read the thesis statements, and for each mark what, how, and why?

1. A new kind of natural resource—bright, innovative workers—will make the difference between a prosperous society and one that stagnates. This creative class of workers will nurture creative cities, invest in creative infrastructures, and create open and secure societies.

   ____

   ____

2. Female leaders can change the course of the political and economic future with their unique values: empathy, community focus, and relational skills.

   ____

   ____

3. The modern plagues of malaria, tuberculosis, and HIV/AIDS pose a major threat to world health and can only be controlled by improving public health conditions in economically deprived environments and improving the mechanics involved in genetic variability that explain the appearance of vaccine and drug resistant strains.

   ____

   ____

Exercise 4B: Creating a Claim or Thesis Statement

Select a new and growing development, technology, or theory in your field of study that interests you. Write a claim that includes the three components of a thesis statement.

What? Health care insured for retired ppl.

How? effeciently improve strategies btw insurance & gov.

Why? retired ppl ↑, maintain their health condition

My claim: lower the price, wider the range of coverage.

Macro Structure

> "I like science writing to be clear and to be interesting to scientists and nonscientists alike. I like it to be smart. I like science writing to have a beginning, middle, and end—to tell a story whenever possible."
>
> —Atul Gawande, M.D., M.P.H.,
> staff writer for *The New Yorker* magazine
> and recipient of the John D. and
> Catherine T. MacArthur Genius Award

In this fast-paced society filled with information, readers expect to easily find a predictable flow or movement of information among the sections of the text. The general macro structure—or "big picture"—readers expect is an **IBC** (Introduction-Body-Conclusion) structure. The IBC begins with an introductory section that provides recognizable information and a starting point and a claim. The main body follows to illustrate and prove the claim with concrete details. A final section or conclusion summarizes and projects possible implications of the claim. Of course, field expert readers of research publications in various disciplines expect a variation of the macro structure. For example, science researchers include an abstract, introduction, methods, and discussion. This adaptation of the IBC structure is used by major science and medical journals for publications.

This section focuses only on the general and common macro structure organizational flow expected by general readers of essays, research articles, and reports. This structure allows readers to immediately know the problem, the importance of the problem, and the claim of the author. Then, the readers can evaluate the evidence presented by the author. By learning to organize the macro structure clearly for general readers, you will establish a solid base of writing that can be adapted and extended for field expert readers. To organize the macro structure of your texts, make sure to include and meaningfully connect the title (reflecting the thesis statement with a unique claim or question), introduction (including a thesis statement or claim), body (justifying the claim in supporting paragraphs), and conclusion (summarizing the significance, predictions, warnings, or calls for action).

Exercise 4C: Analyzing Macro Structure

Analyze the text on pages 53–54, and think about the macro structure. Answer the questions after you have read the article.

1. Use a highlighter to identify these components of the macro structure:
   a. title
   b, thesis statement
   c. body (support with the first justification)
   d. body (support with the second justification)
   e. conclusion
2. Does the title reflect the thesis? How? ______
3. Identify the what, how, and why of the thesis statement.
   What? ______
   How? ______
   Why? ______
4. What is the justification given as support in Paragraph 2?
5. What is the purpose of these transitional words used in Paragraph 2?
   a. *for example* ______
   b. *however* ______
   c. *also* ______
   d. *for example* ______
6. What is the justification given as support in Paragraph 3? ______

7. What is the purpose of these transitional words used in Paragraph 3?
   a. *for instance* ______________________________
   b. *also* ______________________________
8. What does the conclusion do? ______________________________

____

Can Psychology Help the Dismal Science: Economics?

1 To understand why so many individuals choose diets and lifestyles that lead to obesity and ill health, economists typically focus on the usual economic suspects—prices, income, dietary information, and time preferences (the willingness to forego a benefit now for an equal or greater benefit tomorrow). Examination of each variable's role in promoting poor food choices and increasing obesity rates, however, does not typically explain the full story. Standard economics cannot provide the complete answer and should turn to psychology to understand what motivates food choices and health outcomes.

2 Even when standard economics identifies the causes of poor food choices, policymakers have few attractive options to reverse these trends. For example, empirical evidence suggests that rising obesity rates are at least partially attributable to technological advances that have made food relatively cheap, plentiful, and convenient while making expending energy in daily lives less necessary. However, standard economic tools, like using taxes to raise the relative price of unhealthful foods, may have unintended consequences. Taxes on food would disproportionately burden low-income individuals who spend a greater share of their income on food than wealthier consumers. Also, such measures would impose an additional cost for everyone, not just consumers who need incentives to make better choices. For example, they would raise prices for those who are in good health, but who may occasionally enjoy some less nutritious foods.

3 An increasing number of economists look to psychology for answers with findings from behavioral and psychological studies indicating that people regularly behave in ways that contradict basic economic assumptions. People's responses to prices and changes in income, for instance, are not as cut and dry as previously believed. Experimental studies of how individuals pay for various goods and services (e.g., cash versus credit, flat rate versus pay per use) show that payment options influence choices. Time preferences are not solidly fixed either. The tradeoffs individuals make between now and the future fluctuate with situations, stress, and other distractions. Behavioral experiments also reveal surprising findings about how individuals use and process information. Each day, people make thousands of decisions—whether to hit the snooze button on the alarm clock once or twice. They consider whether they have time to eat breakfast at home, and if so, what they should have and how much they should eat. Rather than brood over each and every quotidian task (and make it to work on time), they use simple rules of thumb. Given the sheer volume of information needed to process daily, this is an efficient solution. However, it can lead to systematic reasoning errors that, again, become more likely when individuals are distracted or under stress.

4 For USDA, which devotes considerable resources to nutrition assistance programs like food stamps or school meals, findings from behavioral economics offer alternative strategies that could be applied to improving the diet quality of program participants without restricting their right to choose the foods they like. A thorough analysis of costs, benefits, and potential impacts, however, would be needed before any strategy could be considered as a policy option.

Adapted from *Amber Waves*, June 2007, U.S. Department of Agriculture, www.ers.usda.gov.

Moves in an Introduction

As well as scanning the whole text for a unified beginning, main body, and conclusion, readers search in the introductory section of essays and research papers to discover the general purpose and plan. They look for shifts or **moves** (described by Swales and Feak in *Academic Writing for Graduate Students, 2nd ed.*, Ann Arbor: University of Michigan Press) that show the relevance and importance of the paper.

- **Move 1:** Establish background and context of the claim.
- **Move 2:** Summarize previous research.
- **Move 3:** Show gap between previous research and the focus of your claim (research question raised).
- **Move 4:** State purpose of research.

Exercise 4D: Analyzing Moves in an Introduction

Scan the introduction to an article, and note where each move happens. Write the number of each move after the sentence where it appears in the introduction.

1. Background (context of the problem)
2. Summary of previous research
3. Gap
4. Research question raised
5. Thesis or purpose

Clinical Trials and Novel Pathogens: Lessons Learned from SARS

The recognition of SARS as a transmissible disease prompted international efforts to identify its cause and control its spread. The success of these efforts has been dramatic, with the identification of the SARS-associated coronavirus (SARS-CoV) and the control of SARS outbreaks in all affected countries (1, 2, 3, 4). An evidence-based approach to the management of the patient with SARS is still lacking, however, as no controlled clinical data are available to justify any of the treatments used. If SARS reemerges, clinicians will have little evidence on which to base treatment decisions. Could clinical trials have been conducted during the global outbreak? If so, what steps need to be taken to ensure that such trials are implemented appropriately the next time a similar event occurs. We highlight the challenges faced by researchers attempting to conduct clinical trials of therapeutic agents during an outbreak caused by an unknown or novel pathogen. We focus the discussion on the design and implementation of randomized trials of candidate therapeutic agents, as trials are the gold standard on which therapeutic decision-making should be based. Examples from our own experience attempting to launch a trial of ribavirin therapy for SARS will illustrate these challenges.

References

1. Peiris, JSM, Lai, ST, Poon, LLM, Guan, Y, Yam LYC, Lim, W, et al. 2003. "Coronavirus as a possible cause of severe acute respiratory syndrome." *Lancet* 361:1319–1325.
2. Drosten, C, Gunther, S, Preiser, W, van der Werf, S, Brodt, H R, Becker, S, et al. 2003. "Identification of a novel coronavirus in patients with severe acute respiratory syndrome." *New England Journal of Medicine* 348:1967–1978.

3. Ksiazek, TG, Erdman, D, Goldsmith, C, Zaki, SR, Peret, T, Emery, S, et al. 2003. "A novel coronavirus associated with severe acute respiratory syndrome." *New England Journal of Medicine* 348:1953–1966.
4. Centers for Disease Control and Prevention. "Update: severe acute respiratory disease—worldwide and United States, 2003." *MMWR Morb Mortal Weekly Report* 52:664–665.

From Muller, MP, McGeer, A, Straus, SE, Hawryluck, L, Gold, WL. 2004. "Clinical trials and novel pathogens: lessons learned from SARS." *Emerging Infectious Diseases*. Available from www.cdc.gov/ncidod/EID/vol10no3/03-0702.htm.

Exercise 4E: Text Analysis

Select two published articles in your field written by two different authors for general readers. Mark the new structure components: title, thesis, statement, supporting details for each claim, and conclusion. See pages 51–52 to review. Analyze the introductory sections for the moves.

Credible Support

If readers are to accept your claim or question as believable, they expect specific examples and details as **credible support** that make the general claim concrete and valid. The examples help the readers visualize your claim. The type of support in academic papers will vary based on the field of study, but skilled writers always give good reasons for making their claims. They use examples, statistics, and information from experts on the subject. To help you start thinking about support, follow these guidelines.

1. Paint a statistical picture.
2. Know five leading thinkers in your field.
3. List relevant examples.
4. Find quotations and paraphrases from leading sources.

As you search for credible sources to support your claims, you should make sure the sources are scholarly and reputable. You should become familiar with the publishing companies and journals common in your field of study. When using electronic versions, you should evaluate them cautiously since anyone can post on the Internet. Be sure to check the domains. You can be fairly safe with .edu and .gov domain, but should avoid using blogs, personal websites, or biased sites used for propaganda. You can start your electronic search with *Google Scholar* which will predominantly find peer reviewed articles.

Read this list of 15 news and information sources you can use to read good writing from credible sources.

1. Centers for Disease Control and Prevention (CDC)
2. Journals such as *Science* or *Nature*
3. Library of Congress
4. Mayo Clinic
5. National Academy of Sciences
6. National Geographic
7. *National Public Radio (NPR)*
8. Professional associations such as the American Heart Association
9. *Public Broadcasting System (PBS)* or *British Broadcasting Corporation (BBC)*
10. Smithsonian Institution
11. *Spectrum* online journal (for engineers)
12. The Nature Conservancy
13. Newspapers such as *The New York Times, Los Angeles Times, Wall Street Journal,* or *International Herald Tribune*
14. United Nations (UN)
15. World Health Organization (WHO)
16. Other approved sources (by instructor)

List provided courtesy of J. Greer, University of Alabama at Birmingham.

Exercise 4F: Evaluating Internet Sources

Find four online sources to evaluate for credibility. One should be a general news and information source, and two should be sources specific to your field of study. Evaluate them to determine their credibility. Use the chart to help you compile information to share with your classmates. One has been done for you as an example.

Source/Topic/ Domain	**Date** Less than five years old?	**Author's Credentials** Author considered an expert in the content area, or information affiliated with a reputable organization?	**Peer Reviewed** Article peer reviewed?	**Link Source** Site linked by an academic data base or JSTOR (a non-profit organization)?	**Objective/ Balanced View** Author conducted research and cited sources? Author presented both sides to an argument?
Science Daily Alzheimer's research sciencedaily.com	July 2009 Yes	Information provided by Stanford University Medical Center Yes	Not a published article, but a news article No	A popular, award-winning science news site No	Reported on research findings Yes

Exercise 4G: Finding Levels of Paragraph Support

Analyze the paragraph from *Can Psychology Help the Dismal Science: Economics?* Underline the topic sentence, and use a highlighter to mark the two primary support ideas in the paragraph. Refer to Unit 2, if needed.

> An increasing number of economists look to psychology for answers with findings from behavioral and psychological studies indicating that people regularly behave in ways that contradict basic economic assumptions. People's responses to prices and changes in income, for instance, are not as cut and dry as previously believed. Experimental studies of how individuals pay for various goods and services (e.g., cash versus credit, flat rate versus pay per use) show that payment options influence choices. Time preferences are not solidly fixed either. The tradeoffs individuals make between now and the future fluctuate with situations, stress, and other distractions. Behavioral experiments also reveal surprising findings about how individuals use and process information. Each day, people make thousands of decisions—whether to hit the snooze button on the alarm clock once or twice. They consider whether they have time to eat breakfast at home, and if so, what they should have and how much they should eat. Rather than brood over each and every quotidian task (and make it to work on time), they use simple rules of thumb. Given the sheer volume of information needed to process daily, this is an efficient solution. However, it can lead to systematic reasoning errors that, again, become more likely when individuals are distracted or under stress.
>
> Adapted from *Amber Waves*. June 2007. U.S. Department of Agriculture, www.ers.usda.gov.

Exercise 4H: Searching for Support to Validate a Claim

Find three or four published articles about the new development in your field of study that interests you. Then follow these steps.

1. Find two sources that support your perspective or claim and one or two that present a different claim.
2. Underline the claim or thesis statement in each article, and note the macro structure.
3. Use a highlighter to mark three examples from the support sections that agree with your claim in one color and two that disagree in another color.

Writing Assignment: Outlining Macro Structure with Support

Create an outline of the ideas to support your claim or thesis statement about a research interest area in your field of study. Develop three support ideas to prove your claim, and include at least two secondary levels of details and evidence in each paragraph. Complete the outline.

Title:

Claim or Thesis Statement (include What, How, and Why)

____

____

Point 1 (Topic Sentence)

____

____

- *Expand on the topic sentence with details and examples.*

____

____

Point 2 (Topic Sentence)

____

____

- *Expand on the topic sentence with details and examples.*

____

____

Point 3 (Topic Sentence)

____

____

- *Expand on the topic sentence with details and examples.*

____

____

Concluding Statement

____

____

Exercise 4I: Peer Review of the Outline

Ask a classmate to evaluate your outline by answering the questions and giving you feedback.

1. What question does the writer raise? ______________________________
2. What is the claim? ______________________________

   ____
3. Why is the question important? ______________________________

   ____
4. What three main ideas does the writer use to support the claim? ______________

   ____
5. Do the ideas convince you? ______________________________

   ____

Then adapt your outline based on your reader's feedback.

Title:

Claim or Thesis Statement (include What, How, and Why)

____

____

Point 1 (Topic Sentence)

____

____

- *Expand on the topic sentence with details and examples.*

____

____

Point 2 (Topic Sentence)

____

____

- *Expand on the topic sentence with details and examples.*

____

____

Point 3 (Topic Sentence)

____

____

- *Expand on the topic sentence with details and examples.*

____

____

Concluding Statement

____

____

Creating a Writing Portfolio

Creating a portfolio of the texts you write will help you evaluate your writing skills and become a good monitor of your strengths and weaknesses. As you make note of the features that you find easy and the ones you find difficult, you will increase your skills. Your writing portfolio will contain a collection of all your writings (including first, second, and third drafts) and will be used to discuss, analyze, and evaluate your writing process and developing skills.

The portfolio concept of writing encourages you to think of writing as a process that necessitates multi-drafts, peer and teacher feedback, substantial revision and reflection, and critical thinking skills. It also enables you to examine and evaluate your own development and identify specific areas that need improvement.

You will present the final portfolio at the end of your writing course with a reflection paragraph about each writing assignment, completed rubrics, and a portfolio checklist (in Unit 10). The portfolio should be well-organized and presentable with a "publishable" look for each item.

Writing Assignment: Reflective Paragraph

Write one paragraph reflecting on your writing skills. Reflect on your role as a student, your teacher's role, and your plans. Use these questions to guide you. Take notes before writing your paragraph on a separate piece of paper.

1. Your role as a student: What have you learned? What problems have you confronted? What are your strengths and weaknesses? How much time and preparation have you put into the assignments and class activities? What has been your focus?
2. The role of the instructor: How has he or she facilitated your writing improvement? Which assignments and activities have helped you the most?
3. Your plans for continuing to improve your writing skills: How much time will you commit to writing?

Notes:

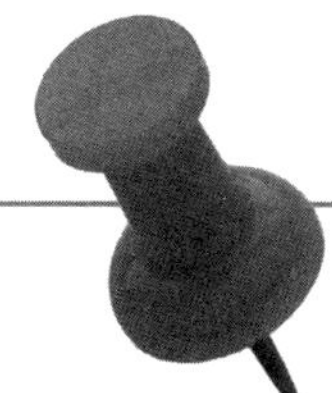

Part 2

Practicing Strategies and Techniques

UNIT 5

Incorporating Outside Sources

"Academic writing in particular calls upon writers not simply to express their own ideas, but to do so as a response to what others have said."

—Gerald Graff and Cathy Birkenstein
in *They Say/I Say: The Moves That Matter in Academic Writing.*
(W.W. Norton & Company, Inc., NY)

As you explore your thoughts and questions about academic and research topics, you will read and analyze the ideas of scholars in published articles and books. You will respond to these ideas, demonstrate your understanding of the claims, and incorporate them into your own writing, which will strengthen your position as a writer. As you restate the words of other writers, you must make sure that you distinguish them from your own words and give credit to the original source. If you fail to do this, it might appear that you have stolen these ideas and have plagiarized—a very serious offense in academia in the United States. In fact, you can accidentally commit plagiarism if your restatement appears too similar to the author's words and syntax even if you cite the source in the text and in the references. To avoid plagiarism, and to work from sources effectively, you will need to master the skills of **paraphrasing, citing sources,** and **summarizing.** You will need plenty of practice, as well as smart planning and discipline, to adequately cover the source work relative to your research question. In this unit, you will practice strategies and techniques for incorporating outside sources and will write a summary of a published article.

Paraphrasing

To support your claims, you will often paraphrase or restate a particular point made by another author in your own words. When you paraphrase, you show the readers that you understand the point or position as you rephrase it without changing the meaning. You also might refute the point to show the validity of your claim. Whether you agree or disagree with the point, you should restate the point with the *exact meaning of the original author without using his or her exact words*. You may have learned that to paraphrase accurately, you should substitute words and phrases of the original source. This is a helpful technique; however, if you only focus on substitution, you may very well plagiarize. You should, more importantly, think critically about the ideas and interweave your thoughts about the passage before attempting to paraphrase.

To avoid plagiarizing, writers should always:

1. read, analyze, and take notes
2. write a one-sentence summary of the article in their own words
3. write the author's relevant points that support or disagree with their ideas in their own words
4. write the reference (source and page number)

Exercise 5A: Analyzing for Plagiarism

Read the two paraphrases of the original source from the U.S. Justice Department website. Which one is plagiarized?

Original Source

Two more defendants pleaded guilty in Milwaukee to charges of criminal copyright infringement as a result of their selling counterfeit software on eBay, Assistant Attorney General Alice S. Fisher for the Criminal Division and U.S. Attorney Steven M. Biskupic for the Eastern District of Wisconsin announced today.

Paraphrase 1

Two additional defendants gave guilty pleas in Milwaukee to accusations of copyright infringement, resulting from their selling counterfeit software on eBay, Assistant Attorney General Alice S. Fisher for the Criminal Division and U.S. Attorney Steven M. Biskupic for the Eastern District of Wisconsin stated today.

Paraphrase 2

The Assistant Attorney General and U.S. Attorney for the Eastern District of Wisconsin announced that two additional defendants admitted guilty pleas when accused of copyright infringement on eBay.

If you selected Paraphrase 1, you are correct because it maintains the original idea in different words and structure, begins with the source of the ideas, and includes an in-text citation.

Exercise 5B: Paraphrasing

Read the text from the Federal Trade Commission website with a classmate. Then write a paraphrase of three or four sentences.

Original Text

Ads and offers for a fake International Driver's License or Permit are showing up on websites and as spam email. They also are sold "on the street" and through storefront operations. The price for one of these fake documents can range from $65 to $350. Many local operations target non-native speakers through ads in foreign-language newspapers that direct consumers to websites or local storefronts. The marketers falsely claim that their documents:

- authorize consumers to drive legally in the U.S., even if they don't have state-issued licenses or if their state-issued licenses have been suspended or revoked
- can be used to avoid points or fines affecting state-issued drivers' licenses; and
- can be used as photo ID in the United States

FTC officials say all these claims are false. In fact, if you are a U.S. resident, and you are caught using an IDP in place of your state-issued driver's license, the consequences can be severe. You could be charged with driving without a license or driving with a suspended or revoked license. If you cannot produce proof of your identity (for example, a valid driver's license, a state-issued identification card, valid immigration documents, or a passport), the officer can assume that you are trying to withhold your identity and arrest you.

Your Paraphrase

____

____

____

____

____

____

Exercise 5C: Practicing Paraphrasing

Read the article. Then answer the questions on page 70.

Bottoms Up: Individualists More Likely To Be Problem Drinkers

1 *ScienceDaily (Nov. 21, 2008)*—What makes residents of certain states or countries more likely to consume more alcohol? According to a new study in the Journal of Consumer Research, high levels of individualism lead to more problem drinking.

2 "We looked at the extent to which consumer levels of individualism (vs. collectivism) were related to their beer and problem alcohol consumption," write authors Yinlong Zhang and L.J. Shrum (both University of Texas—San Antonio).

3 "We found that the higher a region scored on valuing individualism, the greater their beer and alcohol consumption, and this was true even when taking into account the effects of other variables such as income, climate, gender, and religion."

4 The researchers first used archival data to conduct comparisons of beer and alcohol consumption. They compared countries and compared states within the United States. They found that individualism, on a whole-country basis, could significantly predict alcohol consumption. In

the United States, individualism correlated with teen drinking, teen heavy drinking, and adult binge drinking.

5 The researchers went on to manipulate the cultural orientation of individuals in the study. "We did this by simply asking people to either think and then write about enjoying their own life (independent self-construal) or think and then write about enjoying relationships with family and friends (interdependent self-construal)," the authors wrote. "We found that people who were temporarily induced to have an independent self-construal were more receptive to immediate beer consumption than were people who were temporarily induced to have an interdependent self-construal." Study participants did not actually consume beer; they merely indicated whether they felt like it.

6 The researchers found that people with more interdependent mindsets were less likely to over-consume when they were with peers. "The results suggest that people with collectivistic cultural orientations tend to be more motivated to regulate impulsive consumption tendencies than those with individualistic cultural orientations, which in turn makes them less likely to engage in beer or alcohol consumption," the authors conclude.

Adapted from "Bottoms Up: Individualists More Likely To Be Problem Drinkers." (Nov. 2008). *ScienceDaily.* Retrieved from www.sciencedaily.com /releases/2008/11/081117121235.htm.

1. According to the study, who is likely to be a problem drinker? ____________________

   ____

2. What groups did the researchers study?____________________

   ____

3. On a separate sheet of paper, write a short three- or four-sentence paraphrase of Paragraph 5.

Citing Sources

You should insert *in-text citations* as well as a reference list at the end of your text. You can easily show the readers who "owns the ideas" by including signal words and phrases at the beginning of the paraphrase. Some common signal words are listed.

argue	*contend*	*present*	*show*
assert	*explain*	*provide*	*states*
claim	*maintain*	*recommend*	*suggest*

Note these examples.

Winks argues that . . .

While the author asserts that . . . one might debate . . .

Menard contends that . . .

The author presents interesting data on . . .

The theory suggests that . . . .

Even when you insert a signal phrase with the name of the author, you must also include an in-text citation based on the style used by your academic program. Since different communities of writers share a style of documentation, you should follow the guidelines in your field of study. Note the list of possible styles:

American Chemical Society (ACS): http://pubs.acs.org/

American Psychological Association (APA): www.apastyle.org/elecref.html

Chicago Manual of Style: www.chicagomanualofstyle.org

Council of Biology Editors (CBE): http://library.osu.edu/sites/guides/cbegd.php

IEEE Information for Engineering Authors: www.ieee.org/web/pubications/authors/transjnl/index

English/Humanities: Modern Language Association (MLA): www.mla.org/style

---

Exercise 5D: Citing Sources

Select a published article related to your research interest (from your claim on page 51) in Unit 4.

1. Use a highlighter to mark one paragraph that contains an idea that corresponds to your claim or question about the research topic.
2. Write a one-sentence paraphrase of the writer's view using an in-text source acknowledgment:

 ____

 ____

3. Write an in-text citation and bibliographic entry using the source style of your department or school.

 ____

 ____

Summarizing

Similar to paraphrasing, summarizing also requires you to condense another writer's words in your own words. When you paraphrase, you select a particular point of the writer to restate; when you summarize, you state the important points of an article, a chapter, or a book to show your understanding of the writer's message. You might even incorporate paraphrases and quotations in a summary. Since your purpose with a summary is to restate the central points, and not to express your opinion or evaluation, make sure you write an objective and accurate restatement. To summarize correctly, follow these steps:

1. Scan the article by reading the title, abstract, introduction (especially the last sentences), the first two sentences of each section or paragraph, visual illustrations, charts, and graphs, and the conclusion to give you a general idea of the author's views.
2. Read the complete article, and use a highlighter to mark or list only the main ideas.
3. State the overall ideas in this article to yourself.
4. Write a summary in your own words showing the ownership of the ideas by using in-text citations or signal words or phrases.

Exercise 5E: Text Analysis of a Summary

Read the sample summary, and note the highlighted reference signals throughout the summary. Then answer the questions on page 74.

Rosa Morra, post-doctoral fellow (medicine)

The PBS program Newshour (January 28, 2002) reported a debate about the charges of plagiarism brought against two well-known history writers Doris Kearns Goodwin and Stephen Ambrose. The two authors were charged with plagiarism since they used words or sentences from other authors in their books without appropriate use of quotation marks, citations or footnotes. The debate involved several hosts expressing different opinions about the plagiarism issue. **From Jerah Johnson's point of view, a history Professor at the University of New Orleans,** Stephan Ambrose and Doris Kearns Goodwin should not be accused of plagiarism since they did not intentionally use someone else's work as their own. **Johnson remarks** that everybody, including students and professors, can make errors. **On the other hand, the journalist Timothy Noah advocates** that this is a case of plagiarism regarding two academic historians. **He emphasizes** that every freshman at Harvard University takes a course to learn how to avoid plagiarism and believes that a good writer should be well informed on how to write without plagiarizing. **He also strongly believes** that it is necessary to make cases of plagiarism public because a consumer has the right to know what s/he is reading. **Eric Forner, a Professor at Columbia University, agrees with Timothy Noah.** He argues that plagiarism does not depend on the motivation by which writers do it. **He thinks** that at least in Ambrose's case, examples of plagiarism exist since Ambrose has claimed he usually plugs someone else's good story in his own writing. **Eric Forner believes** authors should write carefully to avoid plagiarizing **even though he acknowledges** the difficulty of complete accuracy if an author publishes numerous books per year.

1. Does the writer express an opinion about the issue? Yes No
2. Does the writer only summarize the PBS video? Yes No
3. Does the writer use signal words or phrases? Yes No

Exercise 5F: Reading like a Writer service offers . . .

Before summarizing an article, it can be helpful to read like a writer to clearly understand the writer's intent, organization, and content. Use the chart to analyze the article "Review Blasts Professors for Plagiarism by Graduate Students" in the *Chronicle of Higher Education.* Discuss your ideas with a small group, and fill in the chart.

Questions for Analysis	Observations
Author: 1. Who is the author? 2. Is the author well-known or connected to a reputable organization? 3. Is the article published in a well-respected journal?	Jenifer Couzin-Frankel Science.
Title: 4. What does the title tell you about the audience and purpose? 5. What word in the title captures your attention?	reproduce results service
Purpose: 6. What do you believe is the intent of the author?	eliminate such act
Organization: 7. Who did what, when, where, and why? 8. Can you outline the main sections of the article?	breast cancer biologists work replicate for fee.
Language: 9. Is it written for GRs or FERs?	GRs

Review Blasts Professors for Plagiarism by Graduate Students

Paula Wasley

An investigating committee at Ohio University has called for the dismissal of the chairman of the department of mechanical engineering and another faculty member at the Russ College of Engineering and Technology after finding evidence of "rampant and flagrant plagiarism" by graduate students in the department that took place over more than 20 years. The committee's report is the latest development in the university's continuing investigation of allegations brought by a former graduate student, Thomas A. Matrka, who asserted that faculty members had encouraged or ignored widespread cheating and plagiarism within the department. In March, an academic-honesty oversight committee determined that 37 former graduate students in engineering had plagiarized portions of their theses or dissertations.

This week a two-person faculty committee, appointed by the university's provost to independently review the allegations, has confirmed the extent of the plagiarism. But, while the committee's report censures the graduate students involved, it lays greater blame on faculty advisers who tolerated the students' misconduct.The committee's members—Gary D. Meyer, the institution's assistant vice president for economic development and technology development, and H. Hugh L. Bloemer, an emeritus associate professor of geography—reviewed 55 engineering theses and concluded that seven faculty members in the department had supervised theses that had been plagiarized. The "vast majority of the cases," they wrote, involved three faculty members "who either failed to monitor the writing in their advisees' theses or simply ignored academic honesty, integrity, and basically supported academic fraudulence."

Their report recommended that the provost dismiss the department chairman, as well as a faculty member who had approved 11 plagiarized theses. They recommended that the third professor, who was involved in five of the cases, be placed on probation for two years."We are appalled that three members of the faculty in mechanical engineering have so blatantly chosen to ignore their responsibilities by contributing to an atmosphere of negligence toward issues of academic misconduct in their own department," said the report. "We are amazed to see that the internal ad hoc committee recommended no reprimand for those individuals."

In addition, Mr. Meyer and Mr. Bloemer encouraged the dean of the college to speak with the four other faculty members about the "gravity of their 'oversights,'" requested that the plagiarized documents be removed from library records, and recommended that their authors be required to re-defend their theses again.

More Scrutiny

Their report also recommended further scrutiny of Ph.D. dissertations written by students who were found to have plagiarized their master's theses, and the suspension of three graduate students currently in the department's Ph.D. program until all their work had been cleared of suspicion."You have to respect Hugh Bloemer and Gary Meyer for stepping up to the plate," Mr. Matrka said. "They are the first ones at OU that have actually seriously confronted this." Mr. Matrka, who began collecting evidence of graduate-student plagiarism in 2004 after his adviser told him his own thesis was unacceptable, said that complaints of plagiarism within the engineering college dated back to 1985, but that university administrators had been slow to act on the issue until recently." Some people think that the faculty maybe just had this slip by them," he said. "But when you see two theses with the same title approved by the same professor, with the same first page, I think that speaks for itself."

The university will present the findings of both committees to an outside consultant who is a national expert on academic ethics before taking further action. The consultant, Gary Pavela, is director of judicial programs at the University of Maryland at College Park and a former president of the National Center for Academic Integrity." Academic dishonesty is a critical concern for us," the provost, Kathy A. Krendl, said in a written statement. "This issue reflects on the academic integrity of Ohio University, and it affects the academic and professional careers of students, faculty and alumni."

From The Faculty Section, *Chronicle of Higher Education.* Volume 52, no. 41, page A13. June 16, 2006. http://chronicle.com.

Writing Assignment: Summary

Write a one-page summary of the article about a case of plagiarism and academic honesty published in *The Chronicle of Higher Education.* Include the source in the opening remarks, and use in-text signal words and phrases throughout the summary. Do not include an opinion or evaluation.

Exercise 5G: Peer Review

Ask a classmate to evaluate your summary by highlighting the restated main points and the signal words or phrases that show ownership of the ideas of another scholar, and give feedback. Then answer the questions.

1. Does the writer include his or her opinion in the summary? ____________________
2. Does the writer summarize only the article?____________________
3. Does the writer use enough signal words or phrases? ____________________

Exercise 5H: Evaluating Your Summary

Read your summary, and note the sections highlighted by a classmate and his or her answers to the questions. Follow the suggestions by making the changes. Next, grade the summary using the grading rubric on page 182 that includes the features of a well-written summary. Read the rubric, and ask your instructor to explain any parts you do not understand. Complete the rubric assessing the final draft of your summary. Compare your analysis to your instructors. Compare your grade to your instructor's.

UNIT 6

Process Writing Strategies

"How do I know what I think until I see what I say."

—E. M. Forster, novelist

As researchers and scientists, you will have the opportunity to tell your own "story" about your research and its significance to varied readers. You will narrate, describe, explain, or argue a point of view about the research and write about it. You probably already have a general area of interest or a research subject that you will continue to study and expand; however, as a novice writer, you may find it challenging to get started with a specific focus, claim, or question and create ideas. By modeling a process strategy used by skilled writers, you can begin to create claims distinctive to you and present them to others. As you follow the steps in the process, you will discover what you believe, evaluate your beliefs, adapt and change them, and finish with a quality text. You will use this strategy throughout your writing career. This unit illustrates three stages in the process: **planning, drafting,** and **evaluating and revising** and guides you to create a research interest essay with an IBC structure and appropriate voice and language. The final stage, self-editing, is explained in Unit 7.

Skilled writers begin with an idea that they build and improve as they plan, draft, evaluate and revise, and edit during the writing process. Each writer spends varying amounts of time on each stage of the process, but research shows that professional writers spend a large portion of their time in a particular stage. To compare your writing process to skilled writers, think about the amount of time you spend in each stage and fill in the percentages.

_____ % Planning
_____ % Drafting
_____ % Evaluating and Revising and Editing
100 % Total

Many skilled writers recognize the importance of taking time to plan and develop a strong, unique perspective or focal point. Most of their time is spent in the first two stages.

50% Planning
20% Drafting
30% Evaluating, Revising, and Editing

Of course, the percentages may vary among writers, but they all generally spend more time on planning, evaluating and revising, and editing than on drafting. They like to finish an initial draft as quickly as possible so they can evaluate and reshape their plans, ideas, and language as new ideas develop during this stage. They can spend time on self-editing for sentence-level grammar mistakes, which is an important step to polish the paper professionally and error free. To practice the writing process, you will create a multi-paragraph text about a new research area, development, technology, strategy, or trend that interests you. Read the assignment before starting the process.

Writing Assignment: Research Interest Essay

Select a research area, development, technology, strategy, or trend that you believe will change the future or add to your current research project. Then develop a claim about it, and convince your general readers of the relevance of your claim. Include an introduction, body, and conclusion. Before drafting, read the sample ideas and brainstorm a few of your own ideas.

Sample Innovations or Discoveries (from www.popsci.com)

1. an innovation to speed the diagnosis and treatment of brain injuries of soldiers (by Dr. Shu Yang, University of Pennsylvania professor)
2. a computer beat a human in the game Go
3. a badge that changes color to show extent of brain trauma from bomb explosions
4. a virus that infects other viruses (by French researchers)

Brainstorming Ideas

1.

2.

3.

4.

Planning Stage

After you choose your topic, you will enter the planning stage. In the planning stage, you will search your memory for what you know, investigate published sources, establish a claim and title, and outline your text. You should allow sufficient time for thinking and planning to help you create a fresh or unique perspective about the research area you selected. If you begin to write the first draft without planning, you may have to start over later and eliminate most of your text.

Determining What You Know

Once you have selected the topic of your research interest essay, you should think about what you already know or what you have heard about the topic. Make a list of these things. This will help you as you begin to research published sources on your topic.

Things I Know or Have Read about My Topic

Investigating Published Sources

Search for published sources on the new research area, development, technology, strategy, or trend that interests you. Keep a list of your sources. Look at the sample list of sources and create one from your own research.

Sample Research Publications Notes

"A new state of quantum matter" by Naoto Nagaosa in *Science,* 318 (November 2, 2007) 758–759.

"A steep road to climate stabilization" by Pierre Friedlingstein in *Nature,* 451, No. 7176 (January 17, 2008): 297.

"Does having more physicians lead to better health system performance?" by David C. Goodman and Kevin Grumbach. *Journal of the American Medical Association,* 299, No. 3 (2008): 335–337.

"Gastrointestinal surgery as a Treatment for Diabetes" by David E. Cummings and David R. Flum. *Journal of the American Medical Association,* 299, No. 3 (2008): 341–343.

Research Publications:

After researching what published authors claim about the topic in your field of study or research area, make a few notes on what excites or concerns you.

I truly believe that . . .

I wonder what will develop . . .

How exciting if . . .

A problem that needs to be resolved or addressed about this area is . . .

I question the . . .

Notes

Establishing a Claim and Title

By raising a question about your topic, you can begin to formulate a claim or thesis statement. For example, read the question and the claim (by Anastasia Valecce) it leads to about the influence of Arabic in Argentina.

Research Question: *Has Arabic immigration impacted Argentinean life and contemporary literature?*

How has it influenced Argentina and contemporary literature?

Claim (Answer): *Yes. Arabic has influenced life and contemporary literature in Argentina in three obvious ways.*

You should use the claim to create a title that immediately signals the readers of your unique perspective. For example, the claim about Arabic influence in Argentina becomes the title.

Title: *Arabic Influence in Argentinean Life and Contemporary Literature*

Think about questions that have stemmed from your research about your topic. Use the space to write research questions and claims. Then, write some potential titles.

Research Questions

Claims

Titles

Exercise 6A: Analyzing Questions to Create Claims and Titles

Just as a claim develops from a question, a title should create a question in the reader's mind and indicate a possible claim. Read the list of questions raised by graduate student writers, and create possible claims and titles with a partner.

1. Are we prepared to control the modern plagues malaria, tuberculosis, and HIV/AIDS?

   Claim: ______________________________

   Title: ______________________________

2. Can the optimism about genetically modified foods be questioned?

   Claim: ______________________________

   Title: ______________________________

3. Should individuals be cautious about body scans?

   Claim: ______________________________

   Title: ______________________________

4. Can personalized medicine provide a new direction in cancer treatment?

   Claim: ______________________________

   Title: ______________________________

Outlining

An outline is a preliminary plan for your writing. Outlines help organize the materials and give you the opportunity to list your main points as well as the supporting points for each. When you are ready to create an outline, include the ideas you have generated up to this point. As you write, you will probably add or remove ideas from the outline. Use the sample outline on page 86 to create an outline for the writing assignment you started on page 80.

<table>
<tr><td colspan="2">Title:</td></tr>
<tr><td colspan="2">Claim (Thesis Statement):</td></tr>
<tr><td>Point #1 (Topic Sentence with theme of paragraph). List it.</td><td>Expand on the topic sentence with details and examples. List them.
A.

B.</td></tr>
<tr><td>Point #2 (Topic Sentence with theme of paragraph). List it.</td><td>Expand on the topic sentence with details and examples. List them.
A.

B.</td></tr>
<tr><td>Point #3 (Topic Sentence with theme of paragraph). List it.</td><td>Expand on the topic sentence with details and examples. List them.
A.

B.</td></tr>
<tr><td colspan="2">Possible Conclusion:</td></tr>
</table>

Drafting Stage

The drafting stage allocates time for you to put the ideas from your outline on paper, so you can "see" them as your readers do. The first draft should include the introduction, the body, and a conclusion. Finish the first draft as quickly as possible and stick to your outline to keep you on track. This will allow you time to re-organize and adapt your outline later.

The Introduction

Start by introducing background information to establish your claim and engage your readers in your concept; make sure the information is appropriate for your audience. Include a clear, central claim (thesis) or question that controls the focus and structure of the complete text. Some writers complete the body paragraphs before writing the introduction; however, for practice, first develop the introduction following the moves expected in introductions: background information, previous research, a gap, and purpose of research or claim (Unit 4). You can always return to the introduction and make changes to reflect new ideas that develop as you write the first draft.

Exercise 6B: Introductions

Read the introduction to a sample research interest essay. Then answer the questions about the moves on page 88.

The Forgotten Memories

Fernando Esquivel Suarez, PhD, Spanish

① People generally feel proud when they hear their national anthem or see their flag because these symbols represent a sense of belonging to their nation. ② This phenomenon appears natural to them, but actually an invention caused these feelings, the nation building process (Anderson,1991; Hobsbawn and Ranger, 1983). ③ This process conceptualizes a nation through a common identity and unites different populations under the same state creating symbols and a shared history. ④ For example, in the nineteenth century after the Independence Wars, the learned creoles developed the project of Colombian nation building with their particular perspective of national history and excluded the African-Colombian, indigenous, and working class. ⑤ Currently, many of these excluded ones feel forgotten and disregarded from the national building project with less power and wealth than the Creole national creators (Munera,1998).

⑥ Perhaps, it is time for social researchers to rescue the forgotten memories of the indigenous, African-Colombian, and working class which could be a major step in "remembering" and validating "forgotten" history. ⑦ The starting point for this project should be a rewriting of the celebration of the first centenary of Colombian independence and authenticating the important roles they played.

References

Anderson, Benedict. *Imagined Communities: Reflections on the Origin and Spread of Nationalism*. London: Verso, 1991.

Hobsbawn, Eric, and Ranger, Terence (Editors). *The Invention of Tradition*. Cambridge UK: Cambridge University Press, 1983.

Munera, Alfonso. *El Fracaso de la Nacion: Region, Clase, y Raza en el Caribe Colombiano (1717–1810)*. Bogota: Banco de la Republica, 1998.

1. In which sentence does he mention background and give context for the essay? Sentence _____
2. In which sentence does he include previous research? Sentence _____
3. In which sentence does he consider his audience by defining the research concept? Sentence _____
4. In which sentences does he show a gap? Sentences _____
5. In which sentence does he make his claim? Sentence _____
6. What is the claim? ____

   ____
7. What are the what, why, and how of his claim? ______________________________

   ____
8. Why is his title appropriate? ____

   ____

The Body: Supporting Paragraphs

After completing the introductory section, create supporting paragraphs for each point in your outline to convince your readers that your claim is valid and believable. Remember to begin each supporting paragraph with a topic sentence that focuses the readers on the main idea of the paragraph (Unit 2). Write a draft of your body on a separate piece of paper.

Read an excerpt from the editorial "Turning a Blind Eye" from *Nature Medicine*. Notice the highlighted claim in the introduction and the topic sentences of each body paragraph. The author uses a fairly common and clear organizational pattern for the body section.

■ ■

Turning a Blind Eye

Doctors commonly prescribe drugs approved by the US Food and Drug Administration (FDA) for off-label medical indications. They do so in part based on published clinical studies. Although US law prohibits pharmaceutical companies from marketing drugs for unapproved uses, a draft proposal the FDA issued in October could allow companies to provide medical literature to doctors about off-label uses for their drugs. The proposal falls well short of ensuring that doctors have the right information to decide whether an off-label prescription is appropriate. According to a study in the Archives of Internal Medicine (166, 1021–1026; 2006), 73% of off-label drug uses lack evidence of efficacy. Yet off-label prescriptions make up more than 20% of all prescriptions in the US. Before 1997, pharmaceutical companies had to wait until the FDA approved a drug for a given indication before they could disseminate information about the drug for that indication. However, in 1997, Congress passed the FDA Modernization Act, allowing companies to distribute medical literature about off-label indications to healthcare providers if a number of conditions were met. For example, the articles had to be preapproved by the FDA. Owing to concerns that these conditions restricted free speech, a federal court revoked many of them in 1999 while maintaining that a company could distribute literature to doctors about off-label use of a drug only if the company was planning to submit an application to the FDA for approval of that new use. The existing regulations controlling dissemination of articles lapsed in 2006, so the FDA has now drawn up a fresh proposal.

Surprisingly, this new proposal relaxes restrictions that were previously in place, while also placing excessive trust in the medical literature.

First, the proposal allows for . . . However, medical textbooks are not always peer reviewed and may represent . . .

Second, the proposal calls for . . . However, because companies . . .

Lastly, the proposal does not contain a key element of the previous regulations . . .

Concluding Statement:

The FDA abdicates its advisory responsibilities to the medical community and the general public if it allows recommendations from the medical literature to substitute for regulatory approval of off-label drug uses. If the FDA turns a blind eye to its mission to evaluate safety and efficacy for all the indications for which a drug is used, why do we need the FDA?

Exercise 6C: Analyzing Claims and Supporting Ideas

Read the research interest essay, and answer the questions on page 93.

Green Fluorescent Protein Lights the Future of Biochemistry

Chunfu Xu, Chemisty PhD student

On October 8th, the Royal Swedish Academy of Sciences awarded the Nobel Prize in Chemistry for 2008 to three outstanding chemists, Osamu Shimomura, Martin Chalfie and Roger, for their contributions to the discovery and development of green fluorescent protein (GFP) originally isolated from the jellyfish Aequorea Victoria (1). The intrinsically fascinating and valuable property of GFP, fluorescencing green when exposed to blue light (2), has resulted in a rapid technical revolution in bioscience. Before the application of GFP, scientists could not observe interesting and crucial DNA and protein molecules because of the laggard characterization techniques, which greatly encumbered the development of biochemistry and cell biology. Currently, scientists can simply visualize such previously invisible bio-molecules by tagging GFP to them, which allows scientists to easily monitor the movements, positions and interactions of these crucial molecules by detecting the green light that GFP emits. The discovery of GFP merits the Nobel Prize because it lights the pathway for biochemistry as a marker of gene expression and protein targeting: two important areas in curing gene-related medical problems.

Used as optical highlighters, Green Fluorescent Protein provides a new way to investigate gene expression in living cells. As is commonly known, genes bear the inherited information of almost all creatures including human beings. Neither the biochemical nor the genetic revolution has provided the experimental tools that would allow for well-defined monitoring at the molecular level until the landmark discovery of GFP (2). With modern imaging techniques, scientists can now capture the newly discovered green fluorescence of GFP tagged to DNA molecules. They can track the location and the movement of DNA molecules during gene expression and can understand the process of gene expression. GFP makes it possible to directly watch the pathogenic mechanism of many gene-related diseases, such as cancer and sickle cell anemia. Knowing how these diseases occur can help solve difficult medical problems.

The importance of GFP also lies in its use as a molecular probe to understand many biological processes, especially protein synthesis (2), and detecting the pathogenicity of viruses. Understanding proteins are very important to scientists because they play an essential role in living organisms; no process within cells can carry through without the participation of proteins. In order to actually see those colorless proteins in microscopes, scientists have used dyes and colored antibodies, but these treatments usually involved killing the cell. The discovery of GFP solves this problem that has harassed scientists for centuries; GFP can make many interesting but previously invisible proteins light up under the microscope (3). Thus, monitoring the activities of protein becomes feasible. Furthermore, this new method opens new vistas in detecting the pathogenicity of viruses because proteins construct the most essential parts of viruses. Seen from this angle, GFP also offers new possibilities to defeat HIV, a currently invincible virus.

Green Fluorescent Protein, a gift that nature presents to human beings, greatly accelerates the progress of biochemistry and cell biology. Also, with the help of GFP, we acquire more knowledge about nature and ourselves, especially in the control and therapy of diseases.

References

1. "Green Fluorescent Protein Pioneers Share 2008 Nobel Prize In Chemistry," Oct. 8th, 2008. *Science Daily*, www.sciencedaily.com/releases/2008/10/081008100616.htm.
2. "Scientific Background on the Nobel Prize in Chemistry 2008.The green fluorescent protein: discovery, expression and development." http://nobelprize.org/nobel_prizes/chemistry/laureates/2008/chemadv08.pdf.
3. White, Michael. "Green Fluorescent Protein is Cool, but is it Nobel Prize-Level Cool," Oct. 10th, 2008. www.scientificblogging.com/adaptive_complexity/green_fluorescent_protein_is_cool_but_is_it_nobel_prize_level_cool.

1. What does the title tell you about the writer's belief? ______________________
2. What word in the title captures your attention? ______________________
3. What is the writer's claim in the introduction? ______________________
4. How many supporting ideas does the writer mention in the claim? __________

   ____
5. Does each body paragraph begin with a topic sentence that connects to the claim statement in the introduction? ______________________

   ____
6. Does the writer include in-text citations and a reference list? ______________

   ____

Tone

As you generate the first draft, consider the **tone** that readers "hear" in your writing, the style of emotion you are conveying. Do you present a believable, measured, and careful tone, or do you appear overly confident with your claims about new findings and knowledge? Skilled writers protect themselves from sounding overly certain when presenting new ideas and claims by using formal **hedging markers**. For instance, note that the first claim appears very strong without hedging markers whereas the second claim shows caution and clarity for a claim that might not be true.

Global warming will cause disastrous climate change.

Global warming may cause disastrous climate change.

To protect yourself and to sound credible, you can use verbs and modals.

Sample Hedging Markers	
Verbs	**Modals**
appear indicate seem to suggest tend to to be likely	can could may might

Also, you can select from the formal hedging markers commonly used in academic writing according to Eli Hinkel.

Formal Hedging Markers		
about according to *(+ noun)* actually apparent (-ly) approximately (-ly) broad (-ly) clear (-ly) comparative (-ly) essential (-ly)	fairly likely merely most *(+ adjective)* nearly normal (-ly) partially partly potential (-ly)	presumably relative (-ly) relative to slightly somehow somewhat sufficiently theoretically unlikely

From *Teaching Academic ESL Writing* by Eli Hinkel, published by Lawrence Erlbaum, 2004, p. 323.

Exercise 6D: Using Hedging Markers to Avoid Certainty

Insert hedging markers in the sentences to remove the tone of absolute certainty.

1. Improving lifestyle will prevent diseases.
2. A family history of cancer causes cancer.
3. Scientists and politicians believe that further studies on the nature versus nurture controversy are pointless.
4. Biology's impact on individuals is lasting and unchangeable.
5. Genetically modified crops will stop hunger in the world.

Exercise 6E: Identifying Hedging Markers

Use a highlighter to mark the hedging markers in the text that show the writer is confident but not 100 percent certain.

A Cause of Colombian Violence: The Forgotten Memories

Currently, many of these excluded ones feel forgotten and disregarded from the national building project with less power and wealth than the Creole national creators. Perhaps, it is time for social researchers to rescue the forgotten memories about the roles of the indigenous, African-Colombian, and working class because this exclusion might be one of the roots of current Colombian violence.

The Conclusion: A Final Statement

The final section completes the whole text and should include a restatement of your claim. However, your readers will not be persuaded if you only repeat the claim. By ending with a persuasive statement about the significance, relevance, and importance of your claim, you will leave a positive and convincing impression.

Exercise 6F: Drafting the Text

Create Draft 1 of the research interest essay you started on page 80. Double space the text, use a font size of 11, and include all the parts on your outline:

- Title connected to claim
- Introduction with expected moves
- Body with three supporting paragraphs
- Conclusion with persuasive statement

Evaluating and Revising Stage

After completing Draft 1, you should allow sufficient time for shaping and sculpting the text. Skilled writers revise multiple times because they know that writing is a process of discovery and as they write and rewrite, they create and develop ideas. To see your first draft with a fresh, critical perspective, you should start by evaluating the macro structure of the text for audience, purpose, content, and flow of information between the sections and paragraphs. When you are satisfied that your readers can "see" the overall purpose and structure without having to search for details in the long text, you will evaluate and revise the micro structure for language and flow of information within paragraphs. This evaluating and revising stage allows you to rethink your initial ideas and establish clarity. You should be prepared to revise as many times as needed to present an acceptable final text.

Macro Structure

To evaluate your macro structure, follow these steps:

1. Peruse the whole text and evaluate the introduction, the body, and the conclusion). Do *not* focus on grammar and mechanics at this point.
2. Verify your title and thesis or central claim are connected in meaning. Check to see if you answer what, why, and how in your claim or thesis statement.
3. Make sure your introduction contains the expected "moves" and concludes with your central claim and an indication of how you will organize the text.
4. Read the topic sentence of each paragraph in the body and ensure it connects in meaning to your claim.
5. Study the content in each body paragraph and confirm you have credible and sufficient supporting ideas.

6. Check your claim for hedging markers that convey a tone that sounds knowledgeable and direct but not overly certain.
7. Review your concluding paragraph for inclusion of interesting final remarks.

Exercise 6G: Analyzing Macro Structure

Analyze an excerpt of a text by a medical researcher, and mark the macro structure. Then complete these steps:

1. **Circle** the title and the claim.
2. **Number** the main points in the claim.
3. **Underline** the topic sentence for each supporting paragraph. Make sure the title, claim, and topic sentences connect in meaning.

Malaria, Tuberculosis, and HIV/AIDS: The Modern Plagues: Are We Prepared to Control Them?

Alberto Moreno, MD

> " . . . when the sailors reached these places and mixed with the people there, it was as if they had brought evil spirits with them: every city, every settlement, every place was poisoned by the contagious pestilence, and their inhabitants, both men and women, died suddenly. And when one person had contracted the illness, he poisoned his whole family even as he fell and died, so that those preparing to bury his body were seized by death in the same way. Thus death entered through the windows, and as cities and towns were depopulated their inhabitants mourned their dead neighbors . . . "
>
> —Gabriel de' Mussi, 1348 (7).

The plague or Black Death is how the Europeans named the disease that modified the demographic spectra of the continent in the Middle Ages (7, 8). Centuries have passed and our knowledge about infectious diseases has changed dramatically. The introduction of vaccines and antibiotics and the improvement in sanitation have facilitated the control of several lethal transmissible diseases. Nevertheless, malaria, tuberculosis and HIV/AIDS still have a profound impact on public health and pose a real threat for humankind. A critical question is whether or not the International Health authorities are prepared to face this threat and implement control measures with the development of novel drugs and vaccines. Unless health authorities understand that malaria, tuberculosis and HIV/AIDS have unique characteristics which contribute to their efficacy in transmission and limit their control, even with modern drugs and vaccines, these diseases cannot be controlled. To restrain these diseases, public health officials must consider these features: the improvement in public health conditions; the biological constraints determined by the complex life cycle of the infectious agents; and the mechanisms involved in genetic variability that explain the appearance of vaccine and drug-resistant strains.

The most critical variable to consider is the continued maintenance of transmissible diseases today in economically deprived environments with the control of them requiring a sustained improvement in living conditions . . .

Secondly, new vaccines and drugs cannot control these modern plagues without a consideration of the complex life cycles of the infectious agents. The microbes that cause malaria *(Plasmodium),* tuberculosis *(Mycobacterium)* and AIDS (HIV) contain . . . . . . that represent a biological constraint in the search for the "magic bullet" to effectively destroy them . . .

Finally, the high variability of the infectious agents overshadow the development of vaccines or novel drugs. *Plasmodium, Mycobacterium* and *HIV* have the biological versatility to modify their genetic features . . .

Strategies designed to control malaria, tuberculosis and HIV/AIDS require the implementation of several measures to be effective. Those include the improvement in public health conditions and the development of novel drugs and vaccines. Nevertheless, obstacles still threaten these efforts. Socio-economical conditions forcing the creation of overcrowded slums or migration and deforestation facilitate the spread of such diseases. Furthermore, the complexity of the life cycle and the genetic variability of the infectious agents provide biological constraints for the development of effective drugs and vaccines. The frequent description of failures in the treatment of infected individuals has become the crude reality that illustrates the lack of preparedness of public health authorities facing these challenges. International Health authorities must design a coherent policy as soon as possible that integrates basic science and public health that can significantly impact the control of modern plagues.

References

7. Wheelis, Mark. 2002. Biological warfare at the 1346 Siege of Caffa. Emerging infectious diseases. www.cdc.gov/ncidod/ EID/vol8no9/01-0536.htm.
8. Collins, C.H., Snow, John. 2003. "On the mode of communication of cholera." *Medical Sciences History* 19, 12–19.

Exercise 6H: Peer Review

Ask a classmate to evaluate your research interest essay's macro structure by completing the checklist. Then discuss the analysis with your classmate.

Macro Structure Checklist	✓
After scanning the title, the claim, and topic sentences of each paragraph, I understand the central claim and how it is organized.	
The claim is clear and connected to the title.	
The claim or thesis statement answers *what*, *why*, and *how*.	
Each topic sentenced is connected in meaning to the claim.	
The content in each paragraph is believable and contains outside source signals.	
The conclusion restates the claim and includes the relevance for the future.	

Based on your discussion, write ideas to improve your macro structure.

____

____

____

Micro Structure

After revising the macro structure, return to your text to check the flow of information in each paragraph. Evaluate each paragraph in great detail, sentence by sentence. As you practice and become skilled in connecting sentences, you will spend less time revising the micro structure.

To evaluate your micro structure, follow these steps:

1. Verify that each supporting paragraph begins with a topic sentence that provides the focus.
2. Make sure that transition words are used between sentences when needed.
3. Check that you repeated or substituted words and phrases from sentence to sentence.
4. Confirm that previously mentioned or known information is placed before new information.

Exercise 6I: Revising Draft 1 for Macro Structure

Read Draft 1, and evaluate it based on the steps on pages 96–97. Make any necessary changes and additions to the macro structure as you rewrite. Remember to consider your classmate's suggestions. At this point, do not focus on grammar. Write Draft 2 on a separate piece of paper.

Exercise 6J: More Revising Draft 1 for Micro Structure

Ask a classmate to evaluate your research interest essay's micro structure by completing the checklist. Then, discuss the analysis with your classmate.

Micro Structure Checklist	✓
Each sentence is anchored to the topic sentence.	
Transition words are used between sentences when needed.	
Words and phrases are repeated and substituted from sentence to sentence.	
A logical progression of ideas is established by placing previously mentioned or known information before new information.	

Based on your discussion, write ideas to improve your micro structure.

____

____

____

Exercise 6K: Evaluating Your Research Interest Essay

Read your research interest essay, and note the checklists from a classmate and list of ideas you developed for improving your essay. Incorporate the ideas. Next, grade the essay using the grading rubric that includes the features of a well-written essay on page 181. Read the rubric, and ask your instructor to explain any parts you do not understand. Complete the rubric assessing the final draft of your essay. Compare your analysis to your instructors. Compare your grade to your instructor's.

UNIT 7

Self-Editing: A Survival Skill

"Proofread carefully to see if any words out."

—Author Unknown

Your finished product or final draft should have a level of accuracy to compare as closely as possible to competent writers in your department or program. If not, readers may reject your ideas due to grammatical errors. This means that you should never submit a first draft as your final text but should spend ample time **self-editing** each sentence. Skilled writers usually wait until they complete a first draft before editing at the sentence level since this allows them to develop their creative ideas without interruption from grammar concerns; however, some writers build in this stage of the writing process as they complete individual sections of the text—especially when writing a long text.

This unit presents a basic grammar overview of **writer's grammar** and an **editing classification chart** to help you develop strategies and techniques to self-edit for common problems that many learners face when writing long texts. These are by no means the only problems that you will have as you write various text types, but they are the basic mistakes that will occur frequently if you do not learn to recognize and correct them.

Before we begin the overview, take the quiz to determine what you already know about sentences. Check your answers with a classmate, and use a highlighter to mark those that you do not understand.

Quiz	Answer
List six parts of speech that can be part of a sentence (for example, noun).	adj, adv. v. noun. be.
Highlight the prepositional phrases in the sentence.	Rural areas can compete in today's economy by attracting people in creative occupations to spark growth.
Which is a phase? Which is a clause?	• during the past 100 years • although the landmark was destroyed
List three things you know about word order.	to be ? no pass not - non passive
Name the four sentences types.	question request normal passive
Write an example of an adverb used to begin a clause.	Beautiful as she is.
Write an example of a conjunction used to link ideas.	this paper is good, however, ...

Overview of Writer's Grammar

You do not have to be a grammarian to write well in English, but with an understanding of a few basics, you can learn to self-edit for your frequent grammar mistakes. You can start with recognizing the essential elements that writers use: (1) parts of speech; (2) the core linguistic structure of a sentence (subject + verb + object); (3) phrases and clauses to build complex sentences; (4) a variety of sentence types; (5) academic verb forms; and (6) nouns and articles. Understanding these six fundamentals will help you develop an inventory of your typical mistakes to self-edit and follow your instructor's editing feedback. As you become skilled at finding and correcting these errors, you will learn to make fewer mistakes in your first draft.

Fundamental 1: Parts of Speech

You have probably learned (as you studied for standardized tests such as the TOEFL®) that grammar names types of words in a sentence as parts of speech. We will review these briefly to help you recognize them in sentences for self-editing. Review the list and highlight the ones you recognize.

- **Verbs** (denote existence, action, or occurrence—*The hurricane <u>destroyed</u> the village.*)
- **Nouns** (name a person, place, or thing—*<u>Mary</u> watched the movie.*)
- **Pronouns** (replace nouns or other pronouns—*<u>She</u> speaks slowly.*)
- **Adjectives** (describe a noun—*The <u>bright</u> sunlight filled the room.*)
- **Adverbs** (modify a verb, adjective, or other adverb—*The sun shines <u>brightly</u>.*)
- **Prepositions** (link nouns, pronouns, and phrases to other words in a sentence—*The rocket landed <u>on</u> the moon.*)
- **Conjunctions** (connect words, clauses, or sentences—*Michael studies English <u>and</u> Spanish.*)
- **Interjections** (express a strong emotion or exclamation—*<u>Wow!</u> I am really late to class.*)

Exercise 7A: Recognizing Parts of Speech

Label the parts of speech for each underlined word in the sentences.

American (1) Indians in reservation communities (2) have the poorest health, education, (3) and socioeconomic (4) status (5) of any racial or (6) ethnic group in the U. S. which places (7) them at increased risk (8) for drug abuse and adverse health and behavior (9) outcomes. As nearly half of American Indians women (10) begin child-bearing in (11) adolescence, teen mothers and their offspring are the most vulnerable population (12) at risk. A (13) study with an in-home, paraprofessional-delivered family strengthening curriculum entitled (14) family spirit will focus on this vulnerable group (15) of teen mothers and their children.

1. ________ 6. ________ 11. ________
2. ________ 7. ________ 12. ________
3. ________ 8. ________ 13. ________
4. ________ 9. ________ 14. ________
5. ________ 10. ________ 15. ________

Fundamental 2: Subject + Verb + Object

In its simplest form, a sentence includes a **subject** (usually a noun that states who or what the sentence is about) and a **predicate** (a verb stating the main action of the subject). Of course, these words must make a complete thought and contain meaning.

Babies eat. You can add an **object** (a noun that receives the action and usually follows the verb).

Babies eat **cereal.**

Think about the linguistic structure of your native language. Is it the same as English or different? Analyze the S+V+O sentence. Does the sequence have meaning?

Clouds		reduce		sunlight.
SUBJECT	+	*VERB*	+	*OBJECT*
S	+	*V*	+	*O*

The three words *Clouds reduce sunlight* represent the definition of a basic S+V+O sentence in English. Understanding the core linguistic structure of English sentences will help you to write long, complex sentences (when needed) and edit for mistakes quickly and easily.

Longer sentences are created by adding other parts of speech.

Big clouds always reduce bright sunlight in the morning and afternoon.
ADJ S ADV V ADJ O PREP CONJ

Exercise 7B: Expanding the S+V+O Sequence

Work with a classmate to expand the basic sentences by adding parts of speech.

1. Shakespeare wrote plays. ____________
2. Doctors study diseases. ____________
3. Presidents run governments. ____________

Fundamental 3: Phrases and Clauses

To form meaningful sentences with linking language and information, you need to know the difference between phrases and clauses. A phrase (*along the path, closing the door*) is a group of grammatically linked words *without* a subject and verb, and a clause (*as he finished breakfast*) is a group of linked words containing *both* a subject and a verb. Both phrases and clauses add details and depth to your writing.

Exercise 7C: Identifying Phases and Clauses

Mark whether each item is a phrase or a clause.

	Phrase	Clause
1. providing outdoor recreation in the world		
2. with other partners		
3. the case study demonstrates the commitment to developing regional tourism		
4. since the program began		
5. highlights of the partnership		

An academic sentence may contain a half dozen or more prepositional phrases that add specific and important details. If you find it difficult to recognize prepositional phrases, remember that a preposition is a word that shows a relationship among words, and a prepositional phrase always ends with a noun that is the object of the preposition. A prepositional phrase often functions as an adjective or noun providing details about a noun or verb. To help you understand how prepositional phrases function as adjectives or nouns, ask yourself the questions: Which? What kind? How long? Where? Why? and How?

Note the meaning of the prepositions and the relationship between the underlined nouns.

- direction (You need to turn on the street **to** the west.)
  —*Which street? the street to the west*
- type (You need a book **of** translations before you leave for China.)
  —*What kind of book? of translations*
- place (You can buy that book at the store **at** the corner of Main and First.)
  —*Where? at the corner of Main and First*
- time (He sang **for** two hours.)
  —*How long did he sing? two hours.*
- cause (**Because of** the snow, I took the train.)
  —*Why did I take the train? because of the snow*
- manner (They spoke **with** angry tones.)
  —*How did they speak? with angry tones*

Make sure you recognize the common prepositions listed. Use a highlighter to mark any prepositions that you do not know, and write a prepositional phrase for each.

Common Prepositions				
about	at	by	near	through
above	because of	despite	next	to
across	before	down	of	toward
after	behind	during	off	under
against	below	except	on	underneath
along	beneath	for	opposite	unlike
amid	beside	from	out	up
apart from	between	in	over	with
around	beyond	inside	past	within
as	but	into	since	without

Exercise 7D: Identifying Prepositional Phrases

Place parentheses ( ) around the prepositional phrases, and underline the object(s) of the preposition. Some prepositional phrases may have more than one object.

1. Good local universities will help the development of local economic dynamism as graduates may move to more attractive places.
2. University facilities, high-tech firms, and other creative endeavors have sparked significant growth in urban areas.
3. The presence of a talented creative class of professionals is associated with patent awards, technology adoption, and growth in jobs.
4. People in these occupations seek a high level of life and rewarding work.
5. They are drawn to cities with professional opportunities.

Exercise 7E: Identifying Prepositional Phrases in Your Writing

Analyze the introduction to your article response for the core S+V+O sequence in each sentence. Use a highlighter to mark the subject, verb, and object. Underline the prepositional phrases, and ask a classmate to check your markings. Add two new prepositional phrases to give additional details to your introduction.

Fundamental 4: Sentence Types

You can use clauses to form various types of sentences. Using a variety of sentence types adds complexity to your ideas and helps your readers stay focused. Your readers will lose interest in your text and underestimate your skills and knowledge if you only use one-clause, short sentences and can be confused if you only use long, complex sentences. Skilled writers tend to use short sentences to emphasize an important point and long sentences for details. To construct sentences, you will use two types of clauses:

- An independent clause (main or core clause) can stand alone as a meaningful sentence with a subject and verb. An independent clause is the core of a sentence:

  Avery finished the report.
  S + V + O

- A dependent clause (subordinating clause) cannot stand alone as a sentence. An independent clause must be added to a dependent clause.

  When Avery finished the report, she sent it to the publishers.
  dependent clause + independent clause

To vary sentence structure, you can use the four grammatical types of sentences: **simple**, **compound**, **complex**, and **compound/complex**. Note how each type contains the basic S+V+O sequence in each clause.

Sentence Type	Description and Example
Simple	**Contains one independent clause** A 100-year old famous landmark was destroyed. S V
Compound	**Contains two independent clauses connected with one of seven coordinating conjunctions—*for, and, nor, but, or, yet,* and *so* (FANBOYS)—or a semicolon.** The famous landmark was destroyed, **but** citizens hope S V S V to construct a replica. O The famous landmark was destroyed; the citizens hope to S V S V construct a replica. O
Complex	**Contains one independent clause and one or more dependent or subordinating clauses. The dependent clause is connected with subordinating word: *although, since, because, even though,* etc.** **Although** the landmark was destroyed, citizens hope to S V S V construct a replica. O
Compound/ Complex	**Contains two independent clauses and one or more dependent clauses** **Although** the landmark was destroyed, citizens hope to S V S V construct a replica, **and** government officials plan to O S V designate an historical marker. O

Exercise 7F: Identifying Independent Clauses

Analyze the paragraph from the EPA website for independent clauses by using a highlighter to mark the main or core subject, verb, and object (if included).

The U.S. Environmental Protection Agency

The National Research Council (NRC, 2001) concluded:

Health outcomes in response to climate change are the subject of intense debate. Climate change has the potential to influence the frequency and transmission of infectious disease, alter heat- and cold-related mortality and morbidity, and influence air and water quality. Climate change is just one of the factors that influence the frequency and transmission of infectious disease, and hence the assessments view such changes as highly uncertain. Changes in the agents that transport infectious diseases (e.g., mosquitoes, ticks, rodents) usually occur with any significant change in precipitation and temperature. Increases in mean temperatures result in new record high temperatures and warm nights and an increase in the number of warm days compared to the present. Cold-related stress declines whereas heat stress in major urban areas increases if no adaptation occurs. The National Assessment ties increases in adverse air quality to higher temperatures and other air mass characteristics. However, much of the United States appears to be protected against many different adverse health outcomes related to climate change by a strong public health system, relatively high levels of public awareness, and a high standard of living.

Learn the common words that mark or begin a dependent or subordinating clause. Use a highlighter to mark any you do not know and learn their meanings.

Common Subordinators		
after	so	wherever
although	so that	whether
as	than	which
because	that	whichever
before	though	while
even	unless	who
even if	until	whoever
even though	when	whom
if	whenever	whomever
in order that	where	whose
since	whereas	

A variety of subordinating clauses exist and function as nouns, adjectives, or adverbs.

Type	Description and Examples
Noun Clauses	**function as objects or subjects** I know your name. I know that your name is Emily. *Noun Clause* What they know about the situation is unknown. *Noun Clause*
Adverb Clauses	**function as adverbs modifying verbs** The leader spoke to the union here last week. The leader spoke where the people demonstrated last week. *Adverb Clause*
Adjective Clauses	**function as adjectives modifying nouns** I read two interesting articles last week. The articles that I read last week were interesting. *Adjective Clause*

Exercise 7G: Recognizing Types of Clauses

Use a highlighter to mark the subordinating clauses in the text from the U.S. Department of Agriculture website. Identify the type of clause, and label it as noun, adverb, or adjective.

A 2005 survey by the international food information council found that at least 89 percent of American adults sampled indicated that they believe diet, exercise, and physical activity influence health. These beliefs are reflected in the popularity of books, magazines, and weight-loss programs offering dietary and health advice. Recent consumption statistics, however, show that many of us still choose diets that are out of sync with dietary guidance. Many Americans eat too much sodium, saturated fat, and added sugar yet too few fruits, vegetables, and whole grains with the prevalence of obesity and diet-related illnesses continuing to rise. Although we may intend to have a healthy diet, other preferences often beguile us into food choices that may eventually harm our health. To explain this growing pattern of insidious consumption, economists increasingly turn to behavioral economics—a burgeoning field within the dismal science. Findings from behavioral studies point to a broader set of factors that help determine food choices. These findings also provide an opportunity to begin thinking of new ways to encourage consumers to choose diets better aligned with their own goals for future health.

Writing Assignment: Published Article Response

Write a response of 150–200 words to a recent news article on a research development that interests you (2–3 academic paragraphs). Include a brief summary of the article in your introduction and respond with your belief about the relevance or implications of this new development. Begin your search with *Science Daily* (www.sciencedaily.com) or *Popular Science* (www.popsci.com) for recent developments.

Write for general readers. Give more background, definitions, and explanations than you might give your advisor. **Note:** This is a common task for article, fellowship, or grant writing.

Don't forget to cite the article in your text and give a copy of the article to your instructor.

Exercise 7H: Recognizing and Adding Complexity to Sentence Types in Your Writing

Analyze the sentences in the body of your article response, and complete these steps.

1. Use a highlighter to mark the S+V+O of the independent clauses.
2. Place brackets [ ] around dependent clauses.
3. Underline the subordinators.
4. Tally the types of sentences you use in the essay.

Type	Simple	Compound	Complex	Compound/ Complex
Tally				

5. Focus on your simple sentences. Which are important enough to deserve your readers' focus? Change them to other sentence types to add complexity to your writing.

Rules of Punctuation for Sentence Types

To write clear compound and complex sentences, make sure you use the correct punctuation. Following four rules will help you edit your writing.

Rule	Description and Example
Rule 1	**Always use a comma (,) before one of the seven coordinating conjuctions in a compound sentence (*for, and, nor, but, or, yet, so*).** The famous landmark was destroyed, but the citizens hope to construct a replica.
Rule 2	**Use a semi-colon (;) between two independent clauses without one of the seven coordinating conjunctions.** The famous landmark was destroyed; the citizens hope to construct a replica.
Rule 3	**Place a comma after a dependent clause that precedes an independent clause.** Although the famous landmark was destroyed, the citizens hope to construct a replica.
Rule 4	**Do not use a comma before the subordinating word in a dependent clause that follows an independent clause.** The citizens hope to construct a replica even though funding has not been allocated.

Notice that the example sentences for all four rules have the same context. Compare the examples from the chart and these examples to see how a variety of sentences with similar meanings can be created using the four rules.

Rule 1:

According to a new study, exercise can help produce new stem cells in a mouse's brain, so the mouse might function better as it ages.

Rule 2:

*A new study concludes that Tai Chi might promote better **health; it** could decrease the pain of arthritis.*

Rule 3:

*As the earth's temperatures **increase, scientists** worry about disasters.*

Rule 4:

Visually impaired individuals could move around better if visual robots were available.

Exercise 71: Identifying and Correcting Punctuation Errors

Correct the punctuation mistakes in the sentences.

1. The Allegheny National Forest which is located in northwestern Pennsylvania spans four counties, and is known for its hardwood resources and beautiful fall colors.
2. Even though restoration efforts are an important part of the conservation program in this National Forest many communities do not participate.
3. The Region offers many public and private facilities, camping, fishing, golfing and snowmobiling are the most popular.
4. To attract visitors, a Cooperative International Marketing Initiative has been established with Germany, since many of the early Pennsylvania settlers emigrated from Germany.
5. The initiative will market Tour Packages for German travelers, and will develop catalogues for advertisement.

Exercise 7J: Identifying Sentence Types

Write the sentence type (simple, compound, complex, and compound/complex) in the line after the sentence.

American Indians in reservation communities have the poorest health, education, and socioeconomic status of any racial or ethnic group in the U.S. which places them at increased risk for drug abuse and adverse health and behavior outcomes ① ____________________. As nearly half of American Indians women begin child-bearing in adolescence, teen mothers and their offspring are the most vulnerable population at risk ② ____________________. A study with an in-home, paraprofessional-delivered family strengthening curriculum entitled family spirit will focus on this vulnerable group of teen mothers and their children ③ ____________________.

Exercise 7K: Combining Sentences

With a classmate, form sentences using the scrambled words and phrases in the boxes. Use what you know about parts of speech, word functions, and phrases and clauses to begin grouping words.

also	class	is	mostly	professionals	urban
amenities	creative	it	mountains	rural	while
and	found	lakes	of	settings	with
areas	in	lives	other	the	

Sentence: ____________________

Sentence Type: ____________________

Other Sentences:

____________________ Type: __________

____________________ Type: __________

____________________ Type: __________

class	creative	have	job	people	to
count	end	higher	occupations	proportions	with
counties	growth	in	of	rates	

Sentence: ____________________

Sentence Type: ____________________

Other Sentences:

____________________ Type: __________

____________________ Type: __________

____________________ Type: __________

Sentence Fragments

By making sure that every sentence has a subject and verb and complete meaning, you can avoid writing pieces of sentences or fragments (subordinate clauses or phrases). Avoid mistaking fragments for complete sentences.

Fragment: Because the study was flawed

Complete Sentence: Because the study was flawed, the Editorial Review Board refused to publish it.

Exercise 7L: Identifying and Correcting Sentence Fragments

Underline sentence fragments in the paragraph from the National Archives website, and write them correctly on the lines.

The 19th amendment guarantees all American women the right to vote. Achieving this milestone. Required a lengthy and difficult struggle; victory took decades of agitation and protest. Beginning in the mid-19th century, several generations of women suffrage supporters lectured, wrote, marched, lobbied, and practiced civil disobedience. To achieve what many Americans considered a radical change of the constitution. Few early supporters lived to see final victory in 1920.

____

____

____

____

____

Run-Ons and Comma Splices

By punctuating compound sentences incorrectly, you will make a run-on or a comma splice mistake. A run-on is a sentence with two independent clauses but no conjunction. A comma splice is a sentence with two independent clauses and a comma, but still no conjunction. Read the incorrect samples from the U.S. National Archives & Records Administration website, and compare them to the correct version.

Incorrect: Beginning in the 1800s, women organized, petitioned, and picketed to win the right to vote it took decades for them to accomplish their purpose.

Correct: Beginning in the 1800s, women organized, petitioned, and picketed to win the right to **vote, but** it took decades for them to accomplish their purpose.

Correct: Beginning in the 1800s, women organized, petitioned, and picketed to win the right to **vote; it** took decades for them to accomplish their purpose.

Incorrect: Between 1878 and 1920, champions of voting rights for women worked tirelessly, strategies for achieving their goal varied.

Correct: Between 1878 and 1920, champions of voting rights for women worked tirelessly**, but** strategies for achieving their goal varied.

Correct: Between 1878 and 1920, champions of voting rights for women worked **tirelessly; strategies** for achieving their goal varied.

Exercise 7M: Identifying and Correcting Run-Ons and Comma Splices

Correct the run-on and comma splice errors in the paragraph from the U.S. Health Services website.

> The new privacy regulations ensure a national floor of privacy protections for patients. By limiting the ways that health plans, pharmacies, hospitals and other covered entities can use patients' personal medical information. The regulations protect medical records and other individually identifiable health information, whether it is on paper, in computers or communicated orally. Patients generally should be able to see and obtain copies of their medical records and request corrections. If they identify errors and mistakes. Health plans, doctors, hospitals, clinics, nursing homes and other covered entities generally should provide access to these records within 30 days, and may charge patients for the cost of copying and sending the records.

Subject and Verb Agreement

Understanding sentence types and how to find the core idea in dependent and independent clauses helps you easily self-edit your sentences for another common mistake for novice writers—subject and verb agreement. Subjects that are singular should be followed by a singular form of the verb. Likewise, plural subjects require a plural verb. Locating the subject and the corresponding verb in clauses allows you to verify that the subject and verb agree in number. Read the complex sentence that contains two clauses, and note that the subject and verb in the first dependent clause in brackets [ ] and in the second independent clause in parentheses ( ) agree. By striking the prepositional phrases and identifying each part, you can identify the subjects and verbs easily and make sure they agree.

[As the collective **memory** ~~of older quilt makers~~ **fades**], (new **quilters**
S PP V S

create memories ~~of their own~~.)
V O PP

Exercise 7N: Identifying and Correcting Subject and Verb Agreement

Correct the subject and verb agreement errors. If the sentence is correct, write C after it.

1. Quilt making remain a part of American rural life in the mountains of North Carolina and Virginia even though their popularity has declined.
2. A national revival of interest in quilt making has occurred since the 1970s that have led many women to take it up as a hobby.
3. These new quilters often lacks any family connection with quilts.
4. Instead of modeling their creations upon existing family quilts, quilt makers has turned to books and magazines for examples.
5. The "quilting bee" brings women together to work on a quilt and are such a cherished activity in the popular mind that some writers consider it as a metaphor for democracy.
6. Some mountain native women still consider quilt making a part of their everyday lives.
7. As the collective memory of older quilt makers fade, new quilters create memories of their own, linking the generations with profound respect for traditions of the past.

Exercise 7O: Editing for Subject and Verb Agreement

Edit your article response for subject and verb agreement. Mark each sentence for clauses, subjects and verbs, and prepositional phrases to help you identify the subjects and verbs.

Fundamental 5: Verbs Forms

You probably learned many of the 12 verb tenses from English textbooks, and you might believe that you have to incorporate all the tenses in longer texts. However, research shows that academic writers predominantly use a select few. Research also shows that students frequently apply the tenses inconsistently, creating a lack of unity and textual cohesion which confuses the readers.

Verb tenses are grouped around a time focus—present, past, or future—and an aspect—simple, progressive, or perfect. Look at the conjugation of the verb *investigate* and sample sentences. Use a highlighter to mark the forms that you believe are commonly used in academic writing.

Chart of Verb Tense and Aspect		
Past (Before Now)	**Present (Now)**	**Future (After Now)**
Simple Past *investigated* Mr. Doe investigated the crime for two months in 2003.	**Simple Present** *investigates* Mr. Doe investigates for the state department.	**Future** *will investigate* Mr. Doe will investigate the next case.
Past Progressive *was investigating* Mr. Doe was investigating the crime when the detective was fired.	**Present Progressive** *is investigating* Mr. Doe is currently investigating the scandal.	**Future Progressive** *will be investigating* Mr. Doe will probably be investigating the crime when the trial starts next week.
Past Perfect *had investigated* Mr. Doe had investigated the missing person report for two months when the body was discovered.	**Present Perfect** *has investigated* Mr. Doe has investigated the scandal since 2005.	**Future Perfect** *will have investigated* Mr. Doe will have investigated the crime for five years this time next week.
Past Perfect Progressive *had been investigating* Mr. Doe had been investigating the missing person report for two months when the body was discovered.	**Present Perfect Progressive** *has been investigating* Mr. Doe has been investigating the scandal since 2005.	**Future Perfect Progressive** *will have been investigating* Mr. Doe will have been investigating the crime for five years this time next week.

The three simple tenses and present perfect are the most commonly used. Choose three verbs that are common in your field of study. Fill in the chart with the verb conjugates in the most commonly used forms.

Simple Past	Simple Present	Simple Future	Present Perfect
studied	studies	will study	has studied

Time Frames

Grouping the tenses around the time frames of past, present, and future will help you arrange your ideas consistently at the macro structure and within the paragraphs. When writing about facts and your own ideas in essays and research papers, you will generally use a present time focus throughout the text. When writing literature reviews, case studies, historical analyses, and specific past events or findings, you will use a past time focus. When writing about what will happen in the future, you will use a future time focus. Of course, you can shift from the primary time frame into a different focus, but you will need to mark the change for the readers by using time markers. Note these examples:

today (present)
currently (present)
in 2006 (past)
during the last century (past)
next month (future)
in the next century (future)

Exercise 7P: Identifying the Present Time Frame

Read the paragraph from the U.S. Department of Agriculture website written with a present time focus. Underline all the verbs, and use a highlighter to mark any verbs that shift the focus.

A 2005 survey by the international food information council found that at least 89 percent of American adults sampled indicated that they believe diet, exercise, and physical activity influence health. These beliefs are reflected in the popularity of books, magazines, and weight-loss programs offering dietary and health advice. Recent consumption statistics, however, show that many of us still choose diets that are out of sync with dietary guidance. Many Americans eat too much sodium, saturated fat, and added sugar yet too few fruits, vegetables, and whole grains with the prevalence of obesity and diet-related illnesses continuing to rise. Although we may intend to have a healthy diet, other preferences often beguile us into food choices that may eventually harm our health. To explain this growing pattern of insidious consumption, economists increasingly turn to behavioral economics—a burgeoning field within the dismal science. Findings from behavioral studies point to a broader set of factors that help determine food choices. These findings also provide an opportunity to begin thinking of new ways to encourage consumers to choose diets better aligned with their own goals for future health.

Exercise 7Q: Identifying the Past Time Frame

Read the paragraph written with a past time focus. Underline all the verbs in the paragraph from the National Archives website, and circle the time markers.

Beginning in the 1800s, women organized, petitioned, and picketed to win the right to vote, but it took decades to accomplish their purpose. Between 1878, when the first amendment was first introduced in congress, and August 18, 1920, when it was ratified, champions of voting rights for women worked tirelessly with varied strategies for achieving their goal. Some pursued a strategy of passing suffrage acts in each state—n ine western states adopted women suffrage legislation by 1912. Others challenged male-only voting laws in the courts. Militant suffragists used tactics such as parades, silent vigils, and hunger strikes. Often supporters met fierce resistance. Opponents heckled, jailed, and sometimes physically abused them.

Exercise 7R: Identifying the Future Time Frame

Read the paragraph from the U.S. Department of Agriculture website written with a future time focus. Underline all the verbs in the paragraph, and circle the time markers. The first one has been done for you as an example.

> The last 2 years were marked by a flurry of construction activity in the U.S. ethanol industry, as ground was broken on dozens of new plants throughout the cornbelt, and plans were drawn for even more facilities. As of February 2007, the annual capacity of the U.S. ethanol sector stood at 5.6 billion gallons, and plants under construction or expansion will likely add 6.2 billion gallons to this number. The tremendous expansion of the ethanol sector raises a key question: where will ethanol producers get the corn needed to increase their output? With a corn-to-ethanol conversion rate of 2.7 gallons per bushel (a rate that many state-of-the-art facilities are already surpassing), the U.S. ethanol sector will need 4 billion bushels per year by 2011—roughly twice as much as it consumed in 2006. How the market adapts to this increased demand will likely be one of the major developments of the early 21st century in U.S. agriculture. The most recent USDA projections suggest that much of the additional corn needed for ethanol production will be diverted from exports and feed. However, if the United States successfully develops cellulosic biomass (e.g., wood fibers and crop residues) as an economical alternative feedstock for ethanol production, corn will become one of many crops and plant-based materials used to produce ethanol.

Exercise 7S: Self-Editing for Verb Time Frames

Edit your article response for verb usage by following these steps.

1. Underline all the verbs.
2. Tally the time frames.

Time:	Past	Present	Future
Tally:			

3. Do you need to add time markers to maintain your time frame?
4. Do you use progressive verb forms? ____ Yes ____ No
5. Change progressive verbs to simple.

Fundamental 6: Nouns and Articles

Research shows that mastering the usage of the articles (*a, an, the*) requires time and, perhaps, advanced language skills. Many second language researchers and teachers even state that mistakes with articles are not critical and do not need to be learned early in language study. However, you do not want your proposal, thesis, or dissertation to be rejected by a professor or dean who favors grammatically correct writing. This section will present an overview of article usage to explain the meaning that these seemingly easy words give to nouns. You will not study all the rules for article usage but will begin to simplify these rules, so you can reduce the number of article mistakes in your writing.

To use articles correctly and effectively, you must first understand nouns, a large category of words that name people, places, things, and concepts. Nouns can function in sentences as subjects of verbs, objects of verbs, and objects of prepositions. They are frequently preceded by the articles that give the nouns one of three meanings: definite, indefinite, or generic. As you continue to expand your vocabulary and master the English language, article usage will become easier. For now, let's concentrate on an efficient way to decrease the frequency of article mistakes by learning a few basic concepts of article usage.

Concept 1:

Articles are words that precede and modify nouns by giving them definite, indefinite, or generic meaning.

Type	Description and Examples
Definite **(*the*)**	**Reader and writer share the same knowledge.** Definite meaning is given to a singular or plural noun by using *the*. The windows in this door are broken. The president spoke to the nation.
Indefinite **(*a/an*)**	**Reader and writer do not share the same knowledge.** Indefinite meaning is given to a singular count noun by using *a* or *an*. Every room in this high-rise building has a window. I saw a man rob a bank yesterday.
Generic **(*a/the*)**	**Used for categories, classes, and definitions.** Generic meaning can be given to a singular or plural noun by using *a*, *an*, or *the* before the noun. An astronaut must have years of training. The teacher is responsible for the mental growth of the students. Teachers are expected to be responsible citizens. Corn was the native American's most important crop.

Concept 2:

Singular count nouns cannot stand alone; they must be preceded and modified by an article, demonstrative, possessive, quantifier, or numeral.

I read **a** book. (indefinite article)

I read **the** book. (definite article)

I read **this** book. (demonstrative)

I read **her** book. (possessive)

I read **two** books. (numeral)

Distinguishing between count and non-count nouns might be difficult, but much research shows that academic writers use a limited number of non-count nouns (approximately 32). Learn the nouns listed, and note the non-count nouns commonly used in your field of study. Add those to the list.

Essential Non-Count Nouns		
alcohol	hemisphere	pollution
atmosphere	inflation	prestige
awe	integrity	psychology
biology	intimacy	reluctance
consent	labor	research
equipment	logic	sociology
ethics	mathematics	trade
friction	minimum	traffic
geography	maximum	vocabulary
geometry	navy	welfare
gravity	philosophy	

From *Teaching Academic ESL Writing* by Eli Hinkel, published by Lawrence Erlbaum, 2004, p. 107.

Concept 3:

Plural count nouns can stand alone; they do not need an article preceding them.

Americans consume more and more calories from full-service and fast-food restaurant fare.

Exercise 7T: Identifying Count Nouns and Articles

Underline the singular count nouns in the paragraph from the U.S. Department of Agriculture website. Use a highlighter to mark the articles that modify the noun.

> While spinach and other leafy greens have been associated with numerous food-borne illness outbreaks, the risk of becoming ill from spinach is low. In 2005, U.S. consumers ate 680 million pounds of fresh spinach, and the load of contaminated spinach associated with the outbreak totaled only 1,002 pounds. However, leafy greens are the most likely produce category to be associated with an outbreak. Since 1996, leafy greens have accounted for 34 percent of all outbreaks due to microbial contamination traced back to a specific fruit or vegetable, 10 percent of illnesses, and 33 percent of the deaths.

Exercise 7U: Editing for Articles

Insert five articles missing from the paragraph from the U.S. Department of Agriculture website.

> **Fourth USDA Greenhouse Gas Conference:**
> **Positioning Agriculture and Forestry to Meet the Challenges of Climate Change**
> **February 5-8, 2007—Baltimore Marriott Camden Yards**
> **Baltimore, Maryland**
> **Conference Overview**
>
> Purpose of this conference is to provide forum for presentation of scientific, technical, and policy information related to the impacts of climate change on agriculture and forestry, and potential role of management practices in related ecosystems and product use in mitigating climate change. Ecosystems related to practice of agriculture and forestry are all lands involved in the production of food, feed, fiber, and timber, including croplands, feedlots, pastures, rangelands, forests, and associated wetlands. Conference will feature combination of plenary sessions, technical break-out sessions, and poster sessions organized to maximize interactions, discussion, and dialogue.

Exercise 7V: Identifying Nouns

Underline all the nouns in the paragraph from the U.S. Department of Agriculture website, and identify them as singular count, plural count, or non-count and as definite, indefinite, or generic in meaning. The first one has been done for you as an example.

> Whether eating out or buying carry-out food, Americans are consuming more and more calories from full-service and fast-food restaurant fare. The share of daily caloric intake from food purchased and/or eaten in restaurants has increased dramatically, and the away-from-home market accounts for a large portion of total food expenditures. Analysis of a survey of U.S. consumers indicates that respondents want an enjoyable dining experience, but the desire for health and diet-health knowledge (generic) also play a role.

1. *food/non-count, generic* __________
2. __________
3. __________
4. __________
5. __________
6. __________
7. __________
8. __________
9. __________
10. __________
11. __________
12. __________
13. __________
14. __________
15. __________
16. __________
17. __________
18. __________
19. __________

Exercise 7W: Analyzing Your Writing

Analyze your article response for article usage. Underline all the nouns, and use a highlighter to mark the singular count nouns. Make sure you have an article, demonstrative, possessive, quantifier, or numeral preceding the noun.

Editing Classification

To develop an inventory of your common grammar mistakes, you can use the Editing Classification Chart that has three important categories: sentence structure, verbs, and nouns and articles. Allow sufficient time for the editing stage of writing as you search for mistakes step-by-step. Do not look for all categories as you read your text, but start with Category 1—Sentence Structure. When you complete this category, continue with Category 2. Then, move on to Category 3. As you spend time correcting your mistakes, you will write each new text with fewer and fewer grammar mistakes.

Editing Classification Chart		
Category	**Common Mistakes**	**Write a check (✓) for each section after corrections.**
Sentence Structure	**Sentence Types** • lack of variety (predominantly one type) • confusing complex sentences **Fragments** • phrases or clauses with no complete meaning **Run-Ons and Comma Splice** • incorrect or lack of punctuation between independent clauses	
Verbs	**Time Frame** • inconsistent **Time Markers** • missing or inaccurate **Subject and Verb Agreement** • no agreement with the subject **Verb Forms** • incorrect time or aspect use of less common forms	
Nouns and Articles	**Singular count nouns** • not preceded by an article **Confusing meaning of noun** • definite, indefinite, or generic meaning	

You will also need to search for other types of mistakes before you submit a final draft.

- **Mechanics** (spelling, punctuation, capitalization)

  —You can use the grammar and spell check tool in your word processing program; also, ask your instructor or a friend for help.

- **Word Choice**

  —This is difficult, but as you increase your inventory of academic language, you will improve your word choice. Try using an English ONLY dictionary or thesaurus and ask your instructor for choices.

- **Word Form**

  —This is also difficult, but you can use an advanced dictionary for second language learners to note the correct form based on the function of the word in your sentence: noun, verb, adverb, or adjective.

- **Noun and Pronoun Agreement**

  —Double check all pronouns to make sure they agree with the nouns they substitute.

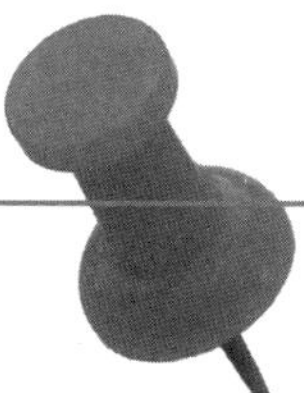

Part 3

Writing as an Insider and Using Common Structures

UNIT 8

Problem-Solution: Multi-Purpose Structure

"What sets you apart as a researcher of the highest order is the ability to develop a question into a problem whose solution is significant to your research community. The trick is to communicate that significance."

—Wayne C. Booth, Gregory G. Colomb,
& Jefferey M. Williams in *The Craft of Research.*
(The University of Chicago Press)

In the final part of the textbook, you will practice writing common structures found in academic writing. While becoming skilled in organizing a variety of text structures, you will also continue to practice the basic qualities of writing using a process of planning, drafting, evaluating, revising, and self-editing. You will start with the **problem-solution structure,** a common and important pattern of research writing for physical and social scientists to identify a problem or issue, examine the problem, and offer solutions or remedies to the problem. For example, in biology the problem may relate to cellular happenings; in literature the problem may involve text interpretation; and in history the problem may involve human events. As a multi-purpose structure, you will find problem-solution texts useful for writing proposals, case studies, essay examinations, reports, research article introductions, grants, and poster presentations.

It is important to recognize that scientists present and solve research problems before real life problems can be resolved. For example, before a cure for malaria can exist, researchers must define problems based on questions about what is not known. Then the knowledge can be applied to treat malaria. However, many research questions might be posed not to solve a real life problem but only to understand literature, art, and, mathematics better—to share knowledge.

Whether you write about theoretical or practical problems, you must observe and describe situations accurately to identify a problem and justify a resolution, and you must also describe the process of the proposed solution and evaluate it. As a novice, academic writer, you may tend to simplify the problem-solution structure stressing the solution more than illustrating the complexity of the situation or context of the problem. This simplification may lead to prescribing the wrong solution or to a lack of interest by the readers.

In this unit, you will write a problem-solution text about a problem you have observed in your field of study related to a class theme. You will describe the problem and evaluate solutions that have already been offered, or you will describe the problem and suggest a novel solution. You will investigate, describe, define, identify, and evaluate—all important skills for academic writers. You will practice these skills following a step-by-step approach as you draft and structure a problem-solution text for clear flow of information.

1. Investigate to learn as much as possible about the problem.
2. Explain your understanding of the specific situation or context including a brief literature survey and details from several outside sources to establish your credentials and knowledge of the research field.
3. Identify or define the problem by raising a question; find a gap in what is known about the situation.
4. Describe a solution for the problem and the steps to be implemented.
5. Evaluate critically how well the solution solves or does not solve the problem; provide the advantages and disadvantages.
6. Conclude by reminding readers of the problem, solution, or implications for future study.

Exercise 8A: Identifying Sections of a Problem-Solution Text

Read the problem solution text and note the sections: situation, problem, solution, and evaluation. Then answer the questions on page 136.

World Hunger and Land Shortages: Is One Solution Hybrid Seeds?

Hengbin Wang

Situation:

World hunger remains a disturbing situation even in the 21st century with rapid discoveries and impressive technology. According to a recent report by the World Health Organization (WHO), the world population consists of one third well-fed, one third under-fed, and the other third starving (1). Half of the hungry people exist in India, forty percent comes from the rest of Asia and Africa, and the remaining ten percent lives in Latin America and other parts of the world (1). Every year, as a result of hunger and its related diseases, more than 5.5 million children around the globe die before they reach the age of 5. What is more, approximately eight hundred million people endure chronic hunger and malnutrition (2).

Problem:

One major cause of the world hunger crisis arises from the shortage of agriculture lands. Food sources come from crops on arable land, which continues to shrink for a variety of reasons. For example, desertification endangers one-third of the Earth with arable land expected to diminish "by two-thirds in Africa, one-third in Asia and one-fifth in Latin America by 2025" (3). One report suggests that China, with its rapid industrialization, will struggle to find land for crops to feed its more than one billion people (4). This shortage of arable land often leads to food shortages, causing wide-spread famine. A Ghana-based Institute for Natural Resources in Africa estimates that Africa might only be capable of feeding twenty-five percent of its population by 2025 due to continuous soil degradation (5). At the same time, the world population keeps increasing. Hania Zlotnik, United Nations Director of the Population Division at the Department of Economic and Social Affairs (DESA) expects the population to increase to 9 billion by 2050 with the major increases in developing countries (6), which means the demand for food will escalate in future decades.

Solution:

Many researchers believe that hybrid seeds can provide an effective solution to this problem. In agriculture, hybrid seed is produced by artificially cross-pollinated plants to improve its characteristics, such as a better yield, more viability under critical conditions, and improved disease resistance. For example, over the last decade, researchers at Kenya´s Agricultural Research Institute (KARI) have developed a new variety of wheat seeds that can survive on the dry lands of East Africa to yield wheat with high productivity (5). These researchers engineered this drought resistance in the hybrid seeds by applying radiation-base technology to modify their genetic properties (5). Farmers now net 20 bags of seed per acre in hot, barren areas previously known as too poor for agriculture, now supply Kenya's families with grains. Researchers originally designed the variety for the lowlands, but the cultivation has also achieved success in the highlands and even in acidic soils.

Evaluation:

From a life-saving pilot program in Kenya, hybrid seeds show their potential for solving the food shortage problem. The high survivability of wheat varieties can provide more cultivable lands and can yield grains with higher productivity and higher quality. In addition, hybrid seeds have more resistance to stem rust—a common epidemic against wheat. However, one shortcoming of the hybrid seeds exists in the absence of genetic variation in their off-spring, which presents a controversy in the area of food and agricultural policy. If a large invasion of pests and diseases occurs, this absence of variation could cause hybrid seeds to be more vulnerable than traditional seeds. Still, this concern could be addressed by promoting traditional seed banks. In sum, while the technology of hybrid seed increases agricultural productivity, more study is needed to help governments create policy that can use hybrid seed to eliminate hunger while also preserving genetic diversity.

References

1. *The world hunger problem: Facts, figures and statistics.* http://library.thinkquest.org/C002291/high/present/stats.htm.
2. Hunger Information. www.freedomfromhunger.org/info/.
3. "Retrospective on Climate Change." *A World of Science, Fifth Anniversary Issue. Natural Science Quarterly Newsletter,* October 2007, page 16. The future of arid lands. http://unesdoc.unesco.org/images/0015/001517/151707e.pdf.
4. Qian, Wang. "Arable land shrinking fast." *China Daily*, June 24, 2009. www.chinadaily.com.cn/bizchina/2009-06/24/content_8316050.htm.
5. "Golden Wheat 'Greens' Kenya's Drylands." *Science Daily,* April 2008. www.sciencedaily.com/releases/2008/04/080430103117.htm.
6. U.N. News Centre. March 11, 2009. www.un.org/apps/news/story.asp?NewsID=30159&Cr=family+planning&Cr1=S.

1. Briefly describe the situation. ______________________________

____

2. What is creating the problem? ______________________________

____

3. What solution does the writer offer? ______________________________

____

4. Does the author believe the solution is viable? How can you tell? ____________

____

____

Stating the Situation

Frequently, beginning writers focus more on the solution than a thorough understanding and analysis of the situation that provides background information on the problem. They find it difficult to see the difference between the situation (background) and the problem. A helpful technique for exploring the situation is to use the five *Wh-* questions: *who, what, when, where,* and *why.*

Answering the five *Wh-* questions allows you to describe the situation and begin identifying the problem.

Exercise 8B: Identifying the Five *Wh-* Questions

Identify the situation in the problem-solution text on pages 134–36 by answering the questions.

1. Who? ______________________________
2. What? ______________________________
3. When? ______________________________
4. Where? ______________________________
5. Why? ______________________________

Identifying the Problem

Identifying the problem requires naming and defining it in specific terms. This means you distinguish the problem from other problems; you discuss the causes and the long term effects; you show where the problem appears, its size, importance, and reasons for eliminating or wanting to solve the problem. Consider these questions as you identify the problem:

1. Is this a real-life, technical, or academic problem?
2. How does the problem connect to the situation?
3. What causes the problem, and what evidence supports these causes?
4. Has anyone attempted to solve it?
5. What happens if the problem is not solved?

Common verbs and nouns in problem-solution writing are listed.

to achieve . . . an outcome	to produce . . . an effect; outcome
to advocate . . . an approach	to prompt . . . a recommendation
to affect . . . an answer	to propose . . . a solution
to answer . . . a problem	to provoke . . . a response
to cause . . . a crisis	to recommend . . . an approach
to contribute to . . . a crisis	to result in . . . a predicament
to create . . . a predicament	to resolve . . . a crisis
to imply . . . a drawback; a cause	to settle . . . an argument
to indicate . . . a source; an answer	to solve . . . a problem
to lead to . . . a solution; a proposal	to stimulate . . . a response

Naming and Defining

As you describe a problem, you will want to define it with terms and concepts that readers can understand. As you read, notice how the authors of the study in *Case Studies in Environmental Medicine* (Centers for Disease Control, 2009) define the concept "disease clusters" in detail. Also, note the extensive outside sources used to establish credibility of the existence of "disease clusters." This detailed explanation could be very helpful in a problem-solution text suggesting that health problems in a specific area could be caused by an environmental situation.

■ ■

Agency for Toxic Substances and Disease Registry
Case Studies in Environmental Medicine (CSEM)
Disease Clusters: An Overview

Definition of Disease Clusters

Unusual <u>events</u> such as clusters occur all the time, especially in large populations. From a statistical perspective, it is almost inevitable that some schools, church groups, friendship circles, and neighborhoods will be associated with clusters of chronic diseases. When first noticed, such clusters are often regarded as resulting from some specific, predictable process, rather than as events with independent causes that happened to have occurred by chance in one particular place (such as a coin toss).

A "cluster" is an **unusual aggregation**, real or perceived, of health events that are grouped together in time and space and that is reported to a public health department (**CDC 1990**). Several breakthroughs and triumphs in infectious disease control have resulted from the epidemiologic evaluation of clusters of cases.

Well-known examples of clusters include the epidemic of cholera in London in the 1850s (**Snow 1965**), the investigation of cases of pneumonia at the Bellevue-Stratford Hotel in Philadelphia in 1976 (**Fraser et al. 1977**), and the 1981 report that seven cases of *Pneumocystis carinii* pneumonia had occurred among young homosexual men in Los Angeles (**CDC 1981**).

Investigations of noninfectious disease clusters have also resulted in notable examples of breakthroughs linking a particular health effect to an exposure, such as angiosarcoma among vinyl chloride workers (**Waxweiler et al. 1976**), neurotoxicity and infertility in kepone workers (**Cannon et al. 1978**), dermatitis and skin cancer in persons wearing radioactively contaminated gold rings (**Baptiste et al. 1984**), adenocarcinoma of the vagina and maternal consumption of diethylstilbestrol (**Herbst et al. 1971**), and phocomelia and consumption of thalidomide (**McBride 1961**).

Disease clusters differ from sentinel events. Sentinel events are occurrences of unexpected diseases or disorders that are known to result from specific, recognized causes of likely relevance to the situation or setting (Joint Commission on Accreditation of Healthcare Organizations 2002). **For example,** the diagnosis of lead poisoning in a child (a sentinel event) should suggest the likelihood of environmental lead contamination that might affect other children. **By contrast**, disease clusters are occurrences of seemingly unexpected diseases for which no immediately apparent recognized cause exists.

Exercise 8C: Analyzing a Problem–Solution Text

Analyze this problem-solution text, and identify the problem section by placing brackets [ ] around it. Do you find a definition in the problem section? If so, use a highlighter to mark the definition, and underline any evidence (outside sources).

Gas-Fueled Tools Can Poison Users

CPWR—Center for Construction Research and Training

Last year, two laborers cleaning an empty underground parking garage in Washington, DC, collapsed and had to be treated in a hospital emergency room for carbon monoxide poisoning. Two other workers and a foreman were also treated. They had been using a gas-fueled power washer.

Workers can suffer carbon monoxide poisoning if they use gas-fueled equipment where there isn't enough fresh air. Even open doors and fans may not provide enough ventilation. In four years, doctors at the George Washington University Medical Center (GWU) in Washington, DC, have seen nine construction workers poisoned by carbon monoxide from using three types of equipment: propane-powered forklifts in a warehouse and gasoline-powered saws and the gas-fueled power washer. Workers using liquid-propane-powered floor burnishers were treated at a hospital in Vermont for the same problem.

Carbon monoxide is an odorless, tasteless, and colorless gas. It quickly enters the lungs and attaches to the blood, which moves it quickly throughout the body. The level of poisoning is affected by the concentration of carbon monoxide in the air, the length of the exposure, the exercise involved in the work being done (which affects the breathing rate), and personal factors. In some cases, a victim may not show dizziness or other symptoms. Unconsciousness or death can result in minutes if the exposure is high. For workers who survive, carbon monoxide can permanently damage the nervous system.

The risk of carbon monoxide poisoning can be cut by using electric or diesel equipment, good ventilation, monitoring, and training. But you need to make sure the solution doesn't add new problems. Electrical equipment should have a ground-fault circuit interrupter to lower the chance of electrocution. Diesel-fueled equipment needs to be properly fitted with filters for diesel particulates in the air that can probable cause cancer. Diesel- and gas-fueled equipment should also be fitted with a catalytic converter and well-maintained, to give off less carbon monoxide.

Even with these steps, the amount of carbon monoxide may still be too high to use the equipment in some areas. Air monitoring is needed to make sure workers are not exposed to unsafe levels of the gas. This monitoring requires special equipment and people trained to use it. Contractors and all workers must also be told about the dangers of using gas-fueled equipment in enclosed spaces. Warning labels can be used. Training can show how to use the equipment safely.

These cases were identified by Dr. Laura Welch and her colleagues at GWU. They have been studying work-related health problems of construction workers treated in the emergency room as part of a special program with the BCTD's CPWR—Center for Construction Research and Training. Funding is provided by the National Institute for Occupational Safety and Health.

This paper appears in the eLCOSH website with the permission of the author and/or copyright holder and may not be reproduced without their consent. eLCOSH is an information clearinghouse. eLCOSH and its sponsors are not responsible for the accuracy of information provided on this website, nor for its use or misuse.

From: *Impact on Construction Safety and Health*, Vol.13, No.1, May 1995.
www. atsdr.cdc.gov/csem/cluster/definition.html.

Exercise 8D: Writing a Definition

Write a short definition of an innovation, new technology, or theory in your field of study. Include outside sources for evidence.

____

____

____

____

____

Cause-and-Effect Relationships

Just as definitions can describe the problem, cause-and-effect relationships can illustrate what produces the problem. To increase the complexity of sentence structure and add variety to a problem-solution text, you can replace common connectors showing cause and effect with *-ing* clauses of result. Read the two sentences illustrating a cause (reason) and an effect (the result).

Cause: *The Federal Government has reduced funding for environmental education.*

Effect: *The lack of funding results in less instruction about the environment.*

Now, notice how you can form more complex structures by using connectors and *-ing* phrases.

Connector: The federal government has reduced funding for environmental education; thus, the schools provide less instruction about the environment.

To form an *-ing* phrase from a clause, drop the subject (*schools*), change the verb to the *-ing* phrase (*resulting in, causing*), and punctuate correctly (a comma is needed after the main clause and the *-ing* phrase)

-ing Phrase: The Federal Government has reduced funding for environmental education, resulting in less instruction about the environment.

Exercise 8E: Using *–ing* Phrases

Rewrite the cause-and-effect sentences by substituting the connectors with an *-ing* phrase and punctuating correctly.

1. Junk e-mail or spam has proliferated dramatically in the past few years; thus, companies have increased costs.
2. Greenhouse gas emissions continue to increase, so the weather patterns change.
3. Political conflict rages worldwide; thereby, millions of refugees become impoverished.
4. The current population is growing; thus, world resources diminish.
5. Humanitarian organizations strive to remove the presence of land mines, so human suffering is reduced.

Describing a Solution

When presenting the solution for either a research or technical problem, you need to describe the process or the steps for implementing the solution—either how the solution can be implemented or how it has been applied. This information has to flow clearly, so another scientist can follow the process and replicate the steps. Notice the flow of information in the solution section of "Gas-Fueled Tools Can Poison Users" from *Impact on Construction Safety and Health,* Vol. 13, No. 1, May 1995). Also notice **bolded** passive voice verb forms in the text. Process texts usually contain passive forms because the person (or subject) who performs the process is not important.

Gas-Fueled Tools Can Poison Users

The risk of carbon monoxide poisoning can be cut by using electric or diesel equipment, good ventilation, monitoring, and training. But you need to make sure the solution doesn't add new problems. Electrical equipment should have a ground-fault circuit interrupter to lower the chance of electrocution. Diesel-fueled equipment **needs to be properly fitted** with filters for diesel particulates in the air that can probable cause cancer. Diesel- and gas-fueled equipment **should also be fitted** with a catalytic converter and well-maintained, to give off less carbon monoxide. Even with these steps, the amount of carbon monoxide may still be too high to use the equipment in some areas. Air monitoring **is needed** to make sure workers are not exposed to unsafe levels of the gas. This monitoring requires special equipment and people trained to use it. Contractors and all workers **must also be told** about the dangers of using gas-fueled equipment in enclosed spaces. Warning labels **can be used**. Training can show how to use the equipment safely.

Also, be careful not to overuse the common words *and, next, or first* repeatedly when describing the steps; use any of the variety of words that signal a process listed.

afterward	eventually	last
at last	finally	later
at the same time	first of all	meanwhile
before this	formerly	previously
currently	initially	simultaneously
during	in the future	

Exercise 8F: *Writing a Short Summary*

Write a short summary about a process you used to complete a lab experiment, a piece of writing, or any other task that interests you. First, list the steps in the process. Then combine the steps into a paragraph that flows well. Avoid common words (*and, next,* or *first*) by using signal markers from the box. Write in the passive voice, so the focus is on the process and not the person performing the process.

Evaluating the Solution

Evaluate your solution(s) critically based on the advantages and disadvantages. This is a central part of a problem-solution text in which you respond directly to the described problem, provide a specific solution, and present the benefits and drawbacks. Think about these questions as you assess and appraise the solution:

1. What is the exact solution?
2. Do you want to discuss more than one solution?
3. What are the difficulties?
4. What are the benefits?
5. What are the outcomes?
6. Will the solution resolve the problem partially or completely?
7. Which solution is preferred (if you present more than one)?

Hedging Markers

You can vary the strength of your statements and opinions by using words that signal degrees of certainty. In promoting or critiquing a solution, make sure you use hedging markers carefully as you present possible consequences of a solution. For example, notice the modal verbs listed and how the degree of certainty varies.

Certainty	**will** This proposal will benefit children's education.
Probability and/ or Possibility	**may** **can** **could** This proposal may benefit children's education.

Use the modal verbs *may, can,* or *could* to make reasonable claims and projections in your problem-solution texts. Refer to Unit 6 to review the list of formal adjective and adverb hedging markers commonly used in academic writing.

Conditionals

If you want to convey a hypothetical or real condition and conjecture in your evaluation section, you can place a conditional or hypothetical meaning on the verbs in the *if* clause. These statements are useful when illustrating the practicality or feasibility of a solution. The examples use a modal in the main (independent) clause.

Hypothetical/Unreal Conditional:

> *This proposal would (could) benefit children's education if the teachers recognized the importance of environmental education.* (Note the past form of the verb in the *if* clause to indicate unreal or hypothetical.)

Real Conditional:

> *This proposal will (may, might, can) benefit children's education if the teachers recognize the importance of environmental education.* (Note the present form of the verb in the *if* clause to indicate a real, possible condition.)

Writing Assignment: Problem-Solution Text

1. As a class, discuss two or three complex problems facing the world today. Select one problem area that affects your lives in particular as students or researchers in a variety of disciplines. Before selecting a problem, read the samples that illustrate how different fields address problems related to global warming.

   Sample Class Theme = Global Warming

   - Math
     —Problem: The number of vehicles on the roads continues to increase, resulting in approximately 32% of $C0_2$ emissions in the U.S.
     —Solution: Math can provide an optimization theory to configure traffic lights to decrease $C0_2$ emissions from cars.
   - Religion
     —Problem: Religious communities do not address the problem of global warming even though they hold the principle of preservation of nature.
     —Solution: Religious communities should establish a working theological foundation against the destruction of nature and utilize religious centers as advocacy against global warming.
   - Medicine
     —Problem: Incineration of medical waste generates gases that add to the green house effect.
     —Solution: Hospitals should create management studies and new varieties of hospital supplies to reduce the type and amount of medical waste.

   Class Theme Selected ___________________________

2. Discuss problems and possible solutions in each of your fields of study connected to the chosen theme.

3. Select a problem in your field of study related to the class theme and "publish" a short text (2–3 pages) with 3–4 outside sources. You will describe the problem and evaluate solutions that have already been offered, or you will describe the problem and suggest a novel solution.

Planning, Drafting, Evaluating and Revising, and Editing

As you learned in previous units, skilled writers follow a path that leads to a well-organized and clear text. As you develop a problem-solution text, follow the steps.

Planning

Research the problem connected to your field of study. Select and print 3–4 articles about the situation. Follow the guidelines from Unit 5 on incorporating outside sources.

1. Read, analyze, and take notes.
2. Write a one-sentence summary of the article in your own words.
3. Write the writer's relevant point in your own words.
4. Write the source, author, publication, and date.

Drafting

Create the first draft of your problem-solution text. Make sure you include outside sources and double space the document.

Evaluating and Revising

Evaluate and revise Draft 1 of your problem-solution text using these steps.

1. Read the draft without stopping.
2. Ask a classmate to read the draft and to answer the questions.
   - What is the problem?
   - What is the proposal for a solution?
   - Is the solution realistic?
   - What should be added to or deleted from the draft?
3. Follow the advice of your classmate and make changes. Rewrite the draft.

Editing

1. Underline all the verbs. Do you maintain a consistent time frame?
2. Use a highlighter to mark all the complex sentences. Place the dependent clause in brackets. Do you find any mistakes with sentence structure?
3. Use a highlighter to mark all the transitions and hedging markers. Have you made appropriate choices for a problem-solution text?
4. Rewrite Draft 2 with as many grammar and vocabulary corrections as possible.
5. Complete the problem-solution rubric on page 182 evaluating your problem-solution text. Compare your analysis to your instructor's.

Complete the chart planning a problem-solution proposal about your field of study. Write 3–4 sentences in each category.

Theme Add topic.	
Situation Describe the general problem and how your field of study connects to the problem or how your field of study can respond to the problem.	
Problem Identify or define a specific problem that your field of study can address. Be specific.	
Solution Describe the solution that you propose. Explain the process of how it works.	
Evaluation Assess the solution objectively and critically. Include the advantages and disadvantages of the proposed solution.	

UNIT 9

Comparative Structure: Advancing the Research Agenda

"Strength lies in differences, not in similarities."

—Stephen Covey, writer

Academic writers frequently **compare and contrast texts**, theories, events, historical figures, scientific processes, and case studies to help the readers see two items more clearly and in a new way. For example, a researcher wants to claim that one theory is more relevant than another, so he or she presents the two theories, describes the similarities and based on categories or criteria for comparing, states why the comparison is important, and explains what can be learned or concluded from the comparison. These structures frequently compare old versus new, traditional versus alternative, high-tech versus low-tech, and invasive versus non-invasive, depending on the field. As you develop a research plan or agenda, it's very helpful to compare and contrast in individual paragraphs or throughout a text.

Exercise 9A: Reading an Example of a Comparative Approach

Read the excerpt from a study illustrating a comparative structure. Notice the comparative words in bold.

A Comprehensive Comparison of Comparative RNA Structure Prediction Approaches

Paul P Gardner, Department of Evolutionary Biology,
University of Copenhagen and
Robert Giegerich, Faculty of Technology, University of Bielefeld

Background

An increasing number of researchers have released novel RNA structure analysis and prediction algorithms for **comparative approaches** to structure prediction. Yet, independent benchmarking of these algorithms is rarely performed as is now common practice for protein-folding, gene-finding and multiple-sequence-alignment algorithms.

Results

Here we evaluate a number of RNA folding algorithms using reliable RNA data-sets and **compare** their relative performance.

Conclusions

We conclude that **comparative data** can enhance structure prediction but structure-prediction-algorithms vary widely in terms of both sensitivity and selectivity across different lengths and homologies. Furthermore, we outline some directions for future research.

Exercise 9B: Analyzing Comparative Structure

Analyze the report from the U.S. Department of Health and Human Services, and answer the questions on page 152 about the two categories compared.

Parents' Concerns

The National Survey of Children's Health (NSCH) asked parents of children aged 5 and under about specific concerns in the areas of speech, language comprehension, manual dexterity, motor skills, behavior, getting along with others, the ability to do things for themselves, and pre-school and school skills. Overall, the parents of almost 37 percent of children reported concerns in at least one of these areas. No variation of reports by location is evident; however, a difference in reports by parents with boys and by families with rising incomes is noted.

Overall, the parents of boys are more likely to report concerns regarding learning, development, or behavior than the parents of girls. Among boys, children in urban areas are least likely to have parents who report concerns (39.9 percent), and children in small rural areas are most likely to cause potential concerns (41.2 percent). Among girls, concerns were also least often reported in urban areas (32.7 percent) but most often reported in large rural areas (35.7 percent).

With regard to family income, parent-reported concerns occur less often as income rises, again with no clear pattern by location. Among children with family incomes below the Federal poverty level (FPL), parent concerns are least often reported in large rural areas (42.5 percent) and most often reported in small rural areas (44.4 percent). Conversely, among children with family incomes of 400 percent of FPL and above, concerns are least often reported in small rural areas (27.8 percent) and most often reported in large rural areas (35.0 percent).

Adapted from "The Health and Well-being of Children in Rural Areas: A Portrait of the Nation," 2005, U.S. Department of Health and Human Services, Health Resources and Services Administration, Maternal and Child Health Bureau.

1. What two categories are being compared? ______________________________

2. Why are these two categories compared? In other words, why are they important to the study? ______________________________

Comparative Structure

Maintaining the structure of comparative texts can be challenging since readers can be confused with the details of the two items between the categories of comparison. To ensure clarity, follow one of two common types of structures referred to as Plan A (Block) or Plan B (Point by Point). In Plan A you present all supporting ideas for one main idea and then all supporting ideas for the second one, creating a block structure. In Plan B, you present each supporting idea and move back and forth between the two main ideas. You will need to consider which plan is more effective to convince the reader of your argument or thesis. Read the thesis, and note the two possible plans the writer can use.

> Contrasting the prediction reliability of biological factors versus nurturing factors <u>in three case studies</u> will show that doctors should first focus on biology when predicting disease risks.

The writer organizes support ideas in two sections, illustrated in Plan A, or in three sections, illustrated in Plan B.

Plan A: Block	
Main Ideas	**Supporting Ideas**
1. **Nurturing Factors** *The writer will discuss each of the case studies comparing the nurturing factors.*	1. Case Study 1 2. Case Study 2 3. Case Study 3
2. **Biological Factors** *The writer will discuss each of the case studies comparing the biological factors.*	1. Case Study 1 2. Case Study 2 3. Case Study 3

Plan B: Point by Point	
Main Ideas	**Supporting Ideas**
1. **Case Study 1** *The writer will discuss Case 1 comparing both nurturing and biological factors.*	1. Nurturing Factors 2. Biological Factors
2. **Case Study 2** *The writer will discuss Case 2 comparing both nurturing and biological factors.*	1. Nurturing Factors 2. Biological Factors
3. **Case Study 3** *The writer will discuss Case 3 comparing both nurturing and biological factors.*	1. Nurturing Factors 2. Biological Factors

Comparative Language

Signal Words

As you have learned, skilled writers always signal the readers as they transition between ideas. By using the signal words of comparison and contrast, you guide the readers to follow your comparative organizational map. Include the words listed when possible.

although	likewise	instead	on the other hand
conversely	in both cases	moreover	otherwise
differs from	in contrast	nevertheless	similarly
even though	in the same way	of greater concern	whereas
however	in no case	on the contrary	while

Exercise 9C: Recognizing Comparative Signal Words

Read the article on the differences between boys' and girls' brains from researchers at Northwestern University, noting the **bolded** comparative signals. Then answer questions on page 155.

Boys' and Girls' Brains Are Different: Gender Differences in Language Appear Biological

ScienceDaily (Mar. 5, 2008)—Although researchers have long agreed that **girls have superior language abilities than boys,** until now no one has clearly provided a biological basis that may account for their differences.

For the first time—and in unambiguous findings—researchers from Northwestern University and the University of Haifa show both that areas of the brain associated with language work **harder in girls than in boys** during language tasks, and that boys and girls rely on **different parts** of the brain when performing these tasks. "Our findings—which suggest that language processing is **more sensory in boys and more abstract in girls**—could have major implications for teaching children and even provide support for advocates of single sex classrooms," said Douglas D. Burman, research associate in Northwestern's Roxelyn and Richard Pepper Department of Communication Sciences and Disorders.

Using functional magnetic resonance imaging (fMRI), the researchers measured brain activity in 31 boys and in 31 girls aged 9 to 15 as they performed spelling and writing language tasks. The tasks were delivered in two sensory modalities—visual and auditory. When visually presented, the children read certain words without hearing them. Presented in an auditory mode, they heard words aloud but did not see them. Using a complex statistical model, the researchers accounted for differences associated with age, gender, type of linguistic judgment, performance accuracy and the method—written or spoken—in which words were presented.

The researchers found that **girls still showed significantly greater activation in language areas of the brain than boys**. The information in the tasks got through to girls' language areas of the brain—areas associated with abstract thinking through language. And their performance accuracy correlated with the degree of activation in some of these language areas. To their astonishment, **however**, this was not at all the case for boys. In boys, accurate performance depended—when reading words—on how hard visual areas of the brain worked. In hearing words, boys' performance depended on how hard auditory areas of the brain worked. If that pattern extends to language processing that occurs in the classroom, it could inform teaching and testing methods.

Given boys' sensory approach, **boys might be more effectively evaluated** on knowledge gained from lectures via oral tests and on knowledge gained by reading via written tests. For girls, whose language **processing appears more abstract** in approach, these **different testing methods** would appear unnecessary. "One possibility is that boys have some kind of bottleneck in their sensory processes that can hold up visual or auditory information and keep it from being fed into the language areas of the brain," Burman said. This could result simply from **girls developing faster than boys**, in which case the **differences between the sexes** might disappear by adulthood. Or, an alternative explanation is that boys create visual and auditory associations such that meanings associated with a word are brought to mind simply from seeing or hearing the word.

While the second explanation puts males at a disadvantage in more abstract language function, those kinds of sensory associations may have provided an evolutionary advantage for primitive men whose survival required them to quickly recognize danger-associated sights and sounds. If the pattern of females relying on an abstract language network and of males relying on sensory areas of the brain extends into adulthood—a still unresolved question—it could explain why **women often provide more context and abstract representation than men.** Ask a woman for directions and you may hear something like: "Turn left on Main Street, go one block past the drug store, and then turn right, where there's a flower shop on one corner and a cafe across the street." Such information-laden directions may be helpful for women because all information is relevant to the abstract concept of where to turn; **however, men** may require only one cue and be distracted by additional information.

1. Does the study show that the differences in boys' and girls' brains appear biological or environmental? ____

   ____

2. What major differences between boys' and girls' brains does the study illustrate?

   ____

   ____

3. According to the article, what implications might these findings have? __________

   ____

   ____

4. What do you think of this study and its implications? Can you think of ideas to argue against the results of the study? ______________________________

   ____

Exercise 9D: Identifying Signal Words

Use a highlighter to mark the comparative signal words in the paragraph written by a PhD student in history.

Prosopography and Microhistory

Daniel Domingues da Silva

Two methods of history research, prosopography and microhistory, are frequently confused and considered to be the same. Although prosopography and microhistory share the same ultimate aim of writing the history of places, people, culture, economy and politics, they differ in scope. Prosopography, on one hand, provides a wider scope than microhistory, observing the past through the behavior of different social groups interacting in the political scenes of a city or country. In contrast, microhistory observes the past through a reduced scope. It tends to see the past following the life trajectory of an individual, how s/he interacts with other individuals of his/her parish, community or town. Thus, prosopography and microhistory conceptualize the scope of an historical narrative in different ways.

Hedging Markers

As discussed in Unit 6, using hedging markers will help qualify your views or generalizations and distance yourself from complete certainty. For example, in comparing nature and nurture, use general statements to identify characteristics about females and males with which your reader might disagree and find exceptions to the generalization. Acknowledge these exceptions to show that they do not occur in 100 percent of the situations.

> "According to a new report in *Psychological Science*, children's temperament may be due in part to a combination of a certain gene and a specific pattern of brain activity."

> "It comes as no surprise that some babies are more difficult to soothe than others but frustrated parents may be relieved to know that this is not necessarily an indication of their parenting skills. According to a new report in *Psychological Science*, a journal of the Association for Psychological Science, children's temperament may be due in part to a combination of a certain gene and a specific pattern of brain activity."

Comparative Claim

In a comparative claim, you tell the reader that you will compare or contrast similar concepts, theories, or articles and indicate the structure of the comparison. You also state the significance of the comparison and include the categories that you will compare. In the sample theses, note that the writers mention the comparative structure for the readers and the categories of comparison or contrast. Providing direction for readers ensures they will know the flow of information early in the paper. Also note that the writers state the implication or reason for the comparison (the purpose).

Chemistry, Biology, Health

Contrasting the prediction reliability of biological factors versus nurturing factors in three case studies will show that ***doctors should first focus on biology*** *when predicting disease risks.*

Education, Liberal Arts, Psychology

In spite of growing emphasis on environmental factors in determining if an individual has mathematical, musical, artistic or athletic ability, evidence reveals that genes may play a more critical part than nurture. Perfect pitch for musicians, myostatin in body builders, and IQ are three factors that can be compared to environmental factors ***to predict the natural ability of individuals.***

History

IQ has been noted as increasing in all countries over the past 100 years. By comparing the history of biological and environmental factors since the early 1900s, evidence will show that ***IQ has increased primarily due to environmental factors.***

Writing Assignment: Comparative Structure Paper

Draft a comparative structure paper using Plan B. Your claim should focus on an area of the "nature vs. nurture" controversy that affects your field of study.

- **Nature View:** Some people believe that gender differences are due to biology (men and women are born differently).
- **Nurture View**: Some people believe that gender differences are due to socialization (men and women learn to behave differently).

Before developing your thesis, think about possible contexts that might interest you about the two views. Read the samples with different views on gender roles.

Women receive less salary than men in managerial positions in academia.

Higher education would improve if more women were represented with top salaries.

Women deserve extra attention to make up for years of subjugation.

Co-leadership is critical in academia.

Men's roles and rights are being threatened by the feminist movement.

Educational organizations will function better if jobs are designated based on innate biological gender differences.

Feminist ideologies blur the differences between men and women and will cause the ruin of education.

Women have been denied leadership positions for too long.

My claim ____

Planning and Drafting

As you create Draft 1, use the claim you made about the nature versus nurture controversy related to your field of study by comparing and/or contrasting the two views. Make sure that you have a valid reason for comparing nature and nurture. For example, in your field of study, men might have higher salaries than women. You might want to illustrate the characteristics that women have in comparison to men that convince the readers that women are actually better suited than men in your profession and, thus, measures should be taken to remedy this lack of equity in pay.

Research the two views related to your thesis, and find several published articles. You must use at least three outside sources.

Source Notes:

Make sure you paraphrase the ideas of published authors and include in-text citations (see Unit 5). Use the preferred method of citation for your field (ACS, CBE, IEEE, MLA, APA), or to simplify in-text documentation for writing assignments in this book, use these styles. Keep the style consistent, and do not switch from one to the other.

- Use reporting verbs (signal phrases) to cite the material

  Walker (2005) states that . . .

- Use a citation after cited material

  . . . which leads to biological differences (Walker, 2005)

Follow the step-by-step approach studied in Unit 6: planning, drafting, evaluating and revising, and editing.

Exercise 9E: Outlining Comparative Text

Outline Plan B structure of your comparative structure paper text using the template. You can substitute world leaders for your field of study (chemists, physicists, religious leaders, biologists, researchers, etc.).

Research Question:

Based on the nature theory, which gender makes better world leaders: men or women?

My question: ______________________________

My answer: ______________________________

Background Information: (state the situation)

Place your claim at the end of the background or introductory section.

Use one of these claims:

By comparing <u>three</u> important characteristics of <u>women and men</u> based on the nature theory, a case can be made that women (or men) will make better ______________ than men (or women).

By comparing <u>three</u> important characteristics of <u>women and men</u> based on the nature theory, a case can be made that ______________ should remain predominantly male/female.

My claim: ______________________________

____

____

Body: Support Paragraphs

Paragraph 1: Begin with a topic sentence about the first characteristic of women from the nature theory (that makes them more effective than men).

or

Begin with a topic sentence about the first characteristic of men from the nature theory (that makes them more effective than women).

First, based on the nature theory, women or men . . .

In contrast, men or women may biologically . . .

My claim: ____

____

____

Paragraph 2: Begin with a topic sentence about a second characteristic.

Additionally, the nature theory portrays women (or men) as . . .

However, men (or women) tend to . . .

My topic sentence: ____

____

____

Paragraph 3: Begin with a topic sentence about a third or final characteristic.

Third, and most revealing, women or men . . .

Of greater concern, men or women . . .

My topic sentence: ____

____

____

Concluding Paragraph: interpret, explain, and summarize your claim; connect the ideas to broader views and to the significance of the claim

My conclusion: ____

____

____

Complete Draft 1.

Evaluating and Revising

Skilled writers know that their best writing occurs by revising multiple times, and they allot time for rereading and reshaping the draft. They know that they must set aside the first draft and return to it later. Then they evaluate the draft as objectively as possible using what they know about good academic writing.

Exercise 9F: Revising

Evaluate and revise Draft 1 with the same mindset as skilled writers by using these steps.

1. Read the complete text, and evaluate the overall comparative organization and the content.
2. Seek feedback from a classmate by asking him or her to scan Draft 1 for content and macro-structure. Discuss suggestions and make any necessary changes.
3. Use a highlighter to mark the comparative signal words or phrases that connect your ideas. Do you need to add any? Yes _______ No _______
4. Underline hedging markers. Do you need to add any? Yes _______ No _______
5. Circle the in-text citations. Do you cite at least one outside source in each support paragraph? Yes _______ No _______
6. Do you include a reference list? Yes _____ No _______
7. Rewrite and reshape Draft 1 as many times as needed based on your classmate's suggestions and your answers to Steps 3–6.

Editing

Once you are comfortable with your thesis, content, and comparative structure, search carefully for grammar and mechanical errors. Before you begin, complete the editing reviews.

Exercise 9G: Editing Review 1

Underline ten grammar errors (fragments, run-ons, agreement, articles, or punctuation) in the paragraph. Correct the errors.

The Smallest Flower in the World

Water-meal is one of the duckweeds in the family Lemnaceae. That contains some 38 species of the smallest and simplest flowering plants. The plant itself average 1/42 inch long and 1/85 inch wide or about the size of one candy sprinkle. It can weigh about 1/900,000 of an ounce, equivalent to two grains of table salt it is very hard to see. If you imagine trying to fill a thimble with them it is estimated that you would need 5,000 plants.

Each Wolffia flower consists of single pistil and stamen; they also produces world's smallest fruit, called a *utricle*. The plant is found in quiet freshwater lakes or marshes with species worldwide. Since the plants have no roots. They can easily float on the surface of the water, where they resemble cornmeals. Water-meal is sometimes used in cold-water aquaria since it is easy to propagate.

Adapted from *Everyday Mysteries: Fun Science Facts*, www. loc.gov.

Exercise 9H: Editing Review 2

Edit your comparative structure paper following these steps.

1. Underline all verbs and time markers. Make sure your time frame is consistent throughout the text with time markers.
2. Use a highlighter to mark the S+V+O order of each main independent clause, place brackets [ ] around the dependent or subordinate clauses, and place parentheses ( ) around prepositional phrases. As you become more proficient with sentence structure, you will not have to do this in such detail, but for now take the time to be thorough. Make any corrections needed.
3. Check punctuation in each sentence to avoid run-ons and comma splices.
4. Check each subject and verb in the independent and dependent clauses to make sure they agree in number.
5. Double underline all singular count nouns; make sure that you have an article, demonstrative, possessive, or numeral before each one.
6. Check all nouns to see if you have given the correct meaning with the proper article: definite (*the*), indefinite (*a/an*), or generic (*a, an, the,* or *Ø*).
7. Rewrite your comparative structure paper for grammar.

When you have completed the revision and editing, grade the paper using the grading rubric on page 183. Compare your grade to your instructor's.

UNIT **10**

Commentary: Participating in Research Dialogue

"The ultimate measure of a man is not where he stands in moments of comfort and convenience, but where he stands at times of challenge and controversy."

—Martin Luther King, Jr.

As you participate in the research dialogue in your field of study, you join a discussion about new and prevailing views and findings. You will be asked to interpret and critique these discoveries and question the strengths and weaknesses of published author's findings and claims. You will engage in discussions about controversial issues for which there is a range of opinions. You will also advocate your ideas and will encounter questioning and skepticism of your claims—a normal part of academic investigation. Some scholars might question one or two details, and others might refute your general claim. If you think of making a claim as basically making an argument, you can understand why others may raise questions and want to verify the data.

This chapter illustrates how to write a **commentary** (an explanation or interpretation) about a new discovery, theory, issue, proposal, or event related to your field of study with a measured tone to show objectivity and credibility. As you develop an argument in response to what others claim, you will develop advocacy and viewpoint writing skills found in grants, book or article reviews, scientific journal articles, scientific essays, and letters to editors. You will present and evaluate existing claims or interpretations, indicate a gap in the research or present something missed or not noticed, and defend your point of view or claim with sound arguments.

Analyzing an Issue

Stephen Rose, Stephen Ceci, and Wendy M. Williams participate in a discussion of the controversial issue of whether scientists should study race and IQ. The three authors present commentaries in articles published online by *Nature*, Volume 457 (*Darwin 200: Should scientists study race and IQ? YES* and *Darwin 200: Should scientists study race and IQ? NO*). Read the short excerpts from the introductory paragraphs of both commentaries.

Commentary 1

Darwin 200: Should scientists study race and IQ? NO

By Stephen Rose
Nature 457 (Nature Publishing Company)
February 2009

The Soviet Union lost a generation of genetics research to the politicization of science when Trofim Lysenko, director of biology under Joseph Stalin, parlayed his rejection of Mendelian genetics into a powerful political scientific movement. By the late 1920s, Lysenko had denounced academics embracing Mendelian genetics, which some said undermined tenets of Soviet society. His efforts to extinguish 'harmful' scientific ideas ruined opponents' careers and delayed scientific progress.

It is difficult to imagine this situation repeating today, when rival views feed the scientific process, and inquiry and debate trump orthodoxy. Yet the spectre of Lysenkoism lurks in current scientific discourse on gender, race and intelligence. Claims that sex- or race-based IQ gaps are partly genetic can offend entire groups, who feel that such work feeds hatred and discrimination. Pressure from professional organizations and university administrators can result in boycotting such research, and even in ending scientific careers.

But hatred and discrimination do not result from allowing scientists to publish their findings, nor does censuring it stamp out hatred. Pernicious folk-theories of racial and gender inferiority predated scientific studies claiming genetic bases of racial differences in intelligence. Even if one does not support such work in the interests of free speech, it should be seen as supporting the scientific process of debate. Important scientific progress on these topics would never have been made without the incentive of disproving one's critics.

"The dominant side goes unchallenged, forestalling the evolution of crucial ideas." There is an emerging consensus about racial and gender equality in genetic determinants of intelligence; most researchers, including ourselves, agree that genes do not explain between-group differences. But some issues remain unresolved, such as identification of mechanisms that bring genetic potential to fruition. Censuring debaters favouring genetic explanations of intelligence differences is not the answer to solving such mysteries.

Commentary 2

Darwin 200: Should Scientists Study Race and IQ? YES

Stephen Ceci and Wendy M. Williams

Are there some areas of potential knowledge that scientists should not seek out? Or, if they do, should they keep the knowledge secret, hidden from the hoi polloi? Certainly Francis Bacon, that great theorist of the birth of modern science, thought so. For with knowledge comes power—potentially dangerous power. In his utopian novel *The New Atlantis*, scholars determined which of their findings were too dangerous to be shared. Modern governments, obsessed with biosecurity, make similar decisions about what can be researched, how, and in what way disseminated. Private companies bind researchers with non-disclosure and confidentiality agreements. Genetic tests for disorders that have no treatment, such as late-stage Alzheimer's, are often not offered for ethical reasons. As Steven Shapin's book *The Scientific Life* documents, the idea of free, untrammelled and publicly-disseminated research, if it ever corresponded to reality, looks distinctly unrealistic today.

To meet the canons of scientific enquiry a research project must meet two criteria: first, are the questions that it asks well-founded? Research based on the assumption that burning coal releases phlogiston fails this test. And second, are they answerable with the theoretical and technical tools available? As the eminent immunologist Peter Medawar pointed out, science is the art of the soluble. Further, given that our society already accepts a number of restrictions to the pursuit of knowledge, it is sensible to require that funded research also addresses questions that either contribute to basic scientific understanding, offer new beneficial technological prospects, or aid sound public policy-making. These criteria are, of course, those used by both public and private funding bodies. So what should we make of the century-old but regularly-recycled call for research aimed at discovering whether there are group differences in intelligence?

Exercise 10A: Investigating and Commenting

Meet with a group of classmates, and answer the questions.

1. What does Stephen Rose believe about scientists studying race?

   ____

   ____

2. What do Stephen Ceci and Wendy M. Williams believe?

   ____

   ____

3. What do you believe? Give a reason for your belief.

   ____

   ____

4. What does *race* mean?

5. Is race for real?

6. What concerns you about the DNA era and possible prejudice? For example: ethnic drugs, IQ testing, the Human Genome

7. What concerns you about using humans (especially minorities and women in developing countries) in experimental drug tests?

Exercise 10B: Timed Writing

Write a paragraph titled "Science Research and Race." You will have 20 minutes to complete the paragraph. When time is up, work with a partner, and discuss your views about science research and race.

Writing Assignment: A Commentary

Write a two-page text positioning a claim about science research and race. Select one article that favors your claim and one that opposes the claim, or select an article that presents both sides. Select one of the topics listed or another one related to your field of study. Make sure your instructor approves your topic.

- tampering with food
- tampering with the environment
- anti-aging or longevity research
- hunger
- biological weapons
- stem cell research
- current proposals to reform health care in the U.S.

Creating a Claim

To make a claim or thesis about science research and race or an issue related to your field of study, consider these questions.

1. What do you believe?

   Should scientists study race and IQ?

2. Do you believe all arguments in favor of the topic?
3. What specific aspect of the controversy interests you the most?
4. What course of action should be taken for your claim?
5. Answer the question *So what?* Why is your claim important?
6. What beliefs do you hold about your topic that can prove your claim?

My claim:

Structuring a Commentary

Construct a commentary with your readers in mind. If you write for field expert readers, make sure you follow the flow of information expected by them. For this writing assignment, include an introduction and a discussion supporting your claim about the issue. Use the common structure in Unit 6 in which you developed a claim with two or three main supporting points and began each paragraph or section with a topic sentence that connects to the "how" of the claim. Follow the template.

Introduction (Situation)

- Describe the current issue.
- Identify the authors involved in the debate (summarize the literature) and their claims.
- Establish a gap in one of the claims (weakness, strength, or inaccuracy)
- Edit your claim if necessary and add it to the introduction.

Despite the fact that Rose makes a convincing argument . . . he could have . . .

This argument provides . . . (1) . . . (2) . . . and (3) . . .

By focusing on . . . , Rose neglected to . . .

If he had . . . , a case could be made that studying race would . . . (1) . . . (2) . . . and (3) . . .

Both Rose and Ceci and Williams maintain interesting views . . . however, they could focus on . . .

By showing . . . (1) . . . (2) . . . (3) . . . ,

Studying race as endorsed by Rose can provide . . . (1) . . . (2) . . . (3) . . .

Studying race as disputed by Rose might result in . . . (1) . . . (2) . . . or 3) . . .

Notes for your introduction:

Discussion (Supporting Paragraphs)

Acknowledge the opposing or agreeing argument either as part of the topic sentence or within the paragraph for each topic sentence.

- Topic Sentence for Supporting Paragraph 1
- Topic Sentence for Supporting Paragraph 2
- Topic Sentence for Supporting Paragraph 3

Write your topic sentences:

Conclusion

Remind your readers of your claim and its significance. Readers will remember your claim and believe your claim if you end with interesting final words.

Note for your conclusion:

On a separate sheet of paper, write a draft of your complete commentary.

Evaluative Words and Phrases

As you participate in this written research dialogue, use evaluative academic phrases and measured words to acknowledge a published author and to show your agreement or disagreement. Note the underlined words and phrases in the sentences, and incorporate them into your commentary.

> Although it is true that genetically modified food reduces hunger, little evidence exists that it is completely safe.
>
> While it is true that genetically modified food can help in specific cases, the fact is that . . .
>
> Despite the fact that tampering with nature has improved society, . . .
>
> In the writer's impressive article, Dr. Howell claimed . . . ; however,
>
> Presenting more cases of plagiarism would have been helpful.
>
> The writer should have provided more . . .
>
> With the writer's innovative yet unconvincing report, . . .
>
> Although the writer's views are interesting and important, she could have presented . . .
>
> Dr. Jones argues that genctically modified food will stop hunger worldwide.
>
> By focusing on the . . . , the author neglected to . . .

Be careful not to overuse the same verbs. Note the variety of the words given in the box.

acknowledge	conclude	describe	explain	oppose
affirm	confirm	disagree	examine	predict
agree	concur	discuss	find	prefer
argue	consider	dispute	illustrate	present
assert	contend	doubt	insist	refute
charge	deny	endorse	maintain	report
claim				

Conditional Verb Forms

When evaluating and commenting on a controversial issue or an author's claim, state what the writer should have done or should do by using the conditional verb forms. Since these forms can be confusing, let's review the basic use of real and unreal conditional forms with examples.

Real or Generally True	If scientists **succeed** in slowing the life process, health costs **will decrease**.
Unreal/Hypothetical: Present	If the life expectancy **increased** by 100 years, society **would change** in many areas. If researchers **eliminated** cancer, the life expectancy **could increase** by approximately three years.
Unreal/Hypothetical: Past	If the author **had discussed** the positive effects of longevity, he **would have been** more persuasive.

Tip Sheet for Revising

When you are satisfied with Draft 1 and the macro structure of your commentary, spend time revising and editing at the micro level. Use the Revising and Editing Tip Sheet.

Revising and Editing Tip Sheet	
Macro Level	**Micro Level**
Self and Peer Review:	**Self Review:**
In the Introduction, the writer:	I use:
___Yes ___No presents and evaluates existing research with in-text citations	___Yes ___No linking strategies within paragraphs
___Yes ___No indicates a gap in the research	___Yes ___No vocabulary appropriate for a commentary
___Yes ___No establishes a claim or research position	___Yes ___No consistent complex structures and sentence variety
In the discussion, the writer:	___Yes ___No verbs correctly (time frame, markers, form and subject and verb agreement)
___Yes ___No begins each paragraph with topic sentence	___Yes ___No articles, pronouns, and nouns correctly
___Yes ___No includes believable details and support	___Yes ___No hedging markers to qualify claims
___Yes ___No includes opposing views and acknowledgement for authors who agree or disagree with the writer's position	___Yes ___No correct punctuation and spelling

Exercise 10C: Peer Review of the Commentary

Ask a classmate to read your commentary and to check for the items listed under macro Level on the Revising and Editing Tip Sheet. Discuss the suggestions with your classmate, and make changes to your commentary.

Exercise 10D: Self-Editing

Use the Revising and Editing Tip Sheet to evaluate the micro level of your commentary. Consider the type of mistakes you have made in previous assignments. Check those areas first.

When you have completed the revision and editing, grade the commentary using the grading rubric on page 184. Then compare your grade to your instructor's.

Portfolio

You will create a writing portfolio to present to your instructor. The portfolio will include a collection of your writings (including all the drafts of the assignments from this textbook). Complete the Self-Review Checklist for the five texts to evaluate your current strengths and weaknesses in academic writing based on the skills presented in this textbook. Write a one-page reflective essay on your current skills.

Self-Review Checklist	
Skill	**Check if Need Review**
Macro Structure IBC Comparative Problem-Solution Commentary	
Micro Structure Topic sentences Transitions Repetition Old versus new information Multiple levels of support In-text source signals	
Claim or Purpose Statement What Why? How	
Introduction Moves Background information Research Gap Claim	
Grammar Sentence structure Verbs Singular/plural Agreement Articles Formal language use Hedging markers Punctuation	

Appendixes

Grading Criteria

	4 Points Excellent to Very Good	3 Points Good to Average	2 Points Unsatisfactory	1 Point Unsatisfactory
Audience and Purpose	Clear, focused, and persuasive thesis. Shows clear awareness of intended audience.	Clearly stated thesis. Shows some awareness of intended audience.	May lack a thesis or purpose is not clear. Shows very little awareness of intended audience.	May lack a thesis or purpose is not clear. Shows almost no awareness of intended audience.
Content and Support	Fully developed ideas. Concrete and credible supporting details. Substantive development of thesis. Demonstration of knowledge of subject.	Adequate content and details but may lack development of thesis and persuasion at times.	Support generally lacks details that are perceptive and persuasive.	Ideas are not developed or persuasive.
Organization and Unity (Macro Level)	A very clear and visual organizational plan. Title, thesis, and topic sentences are clearly connected. Very effective concluding ideas with prediction, warning, or call for action.	Clear organizational plan with no more than one paragraph unrelated to the organizational plan. Title, thesis, and topic sentences are generally connected. Clear concluding ideas.	Organization may be unclear or confusing. Lacks connection between thesis and main ideas. Concluding ideas only restate the thesis.	Has no organizational plan or central idea.
Flow of Information and Cohesion (Micro Level)	Ideas within paragraphs are well-connected with transitions and other cohesive devices.	Ideas within paragraph are generally connected with transitions and other cohesive devices.	Lacks connections between ideas causing difficulty in following focus of the paragraphs.	Almost no connections between ideas. The focus of the paragraphs cannot be followed.
Grammar and Language Use	Consistent use of complex structures. Few errors of tense, agreement, and word order. Correct use of articles, pronouns, and nouns. Language use appropriate for formal, academic writing	Some use of complex structures. Shows appropriate use of grammar but with a variety of grammar mistakes. Language use appropriate but may include informal usage.	Sentences are simple and often incomplete with patterned grammar mistakes. Language use is predominantly informal.	Contains consistent grammar and language usage errors that obscure the meaning.
Mechanics and Proofreading	Clearly punctuated with evidence of editing and proofreading.	Most sentences are complete and correctly punctuated with some evidence of editing and proofreading.	Some sentences are complete and correctly punctuated with very little evidence of editing or proofreading.	No evidence of editing or proofreading.

Grading Rubric: Biographical Statement

Content	Points			
Purpose	4 (A)	3 (B)	2 (C)	1 (D)
States unique theme in first paragraph				
Support	4	3	2	1
Uses primary and secondary levels of support throughout				
Organization and Unity	4	3	2	1
Includes topic sentences that show the specific focus of each paragraph				
Total Points (12 possible): _______ **Grade (Percentage):** _______				

Grading Rubric: Summary

Guidelines	✓
Submitted by due date	
Double-spaced	
One page	

Content	Points			
Summary	4 (A)	3 (B)	2 (C)	1(D)
Fully identifies the original sources				
Includes only main ideas of the sources (without personal opinion)				
Restates the original ideas without exact words of author				
Uses effective signal phrases to reference sources throughout the summary				
Uses formal, academic language				
Total Points (20 possible): _______ **Grade (Percentage):** _______				

Grading Rubric: Research Interest Essay

Guidelines	✓
Submitted by due date	
Double-spaced	
Approximately two pages (11 point font)	

Content	Points			
Audience and Purpose	4 (A)	3 (B)	2 (C)	1(D)
Has clear intended audience				
Contains persuasive thesis, reflects unique claim				
Support	4	3	2	1
Includes believable support				
Contains appropriate multi-levels of support				
Uses in-text source signals				
Flow of Information at Macro Level	4	3	2	1
Uses basic IBC structure				
Has a title that connects to the thesis				
Includes an introduction with well-mapped ideas or moves				
Contains supporting paragraphs with topic sentences				
Includes a concluding idea with significance, prediction, warning, or call for action				
Flow of Information at Micro Level	4	3	2	1
Employs linking strategies (words and phrases) to connect ideas within sentences and between sentences in paragraphs				
Total Points (44 possible): ______ **Grade (Percentage):** ______				

Grading Rubric: Problem-Solution Text

Guidelines	✓
Submitted by due date	
Double-spaced	
Approximately two pages (11-point font)	

Content	**Points**			
Audience and Purpose	4 (A)	3 (B)	2 (C)	1 (D)
Has clear intended audience				
Contains the problem–solution text purpose, reflects unique claim				
Content and Support	4	3	2	1
Includes believable support				
Contains appropriate multi-levels of support				
Uses in-text source signals				
Flow of Information at Macro Level	4	3	2	1
Follows basic structure of a problem-solution text : (1) *Describes* a situation; (2) *Identifies* a problem; (3) *Describes* a Solution; (4) *Evaluates* the Solution				
Has a title that connects to the thesis and the introduction includes well-mapped ideas or moves				
Contains supporting paragraphs with topic sentences				
Includes concluding idea with significance, prediction, warning, or call for action				
Flow of Information at Micro Level	4	3	2	1
Employs linking strategies (words, phrases, punctuation) to connect ideas within sentences and between sentences in paragraphs				
Grammar and Language Use	4	3	2	1
Uses a range of academic vocabulary appropriate for formal, academic writing and problem–solution text				
Maintains consistent use of complex structures and a variety of sentence types				
Uses correct verbs (time frame, markers, form, and subject and verb agreement)				
Uses correct articles, pronouns, and nouns				
Employs hedging markers to qualify claim				
Mechanics	4	3	2	1
Uses correct punctuation with evidence of editing and proofreading				

Total Points (64 possible): _______
Grade (Percentage): _______

Grading Rubric: Comparative Structure Paper

Guidelines	✓
Submitted by due date	
Double-spaced	
Approximately two pages (11-point font)	

Content	Points			
Audience and Purpose	4 (A)	3 (B)	2 (C)	1 (D)
Has clear intended audience				
Contains clear persuasive thesis, reflects unique claim				
Content and Support	4	3	2	1
Includes believable support				
Contains appropriate multi-levels of support				
Uses in-text source signals				
Flow of Information at Macro Level	4	3	2	1
Uses comparative structure				
Has a title that connects to the thesis and the introduction includes well-mapped ideas or moves				
Contains supporting paragraphs with topic sentences				
Includes a concluding idea with significance, prediction, warning, or call for action				
Flow of Information at Micro Level	4	3	2	1
Employs linking strategies (words, phrases, and punctuation) to connect ideas within sentences and between sentences in paragraphs				
Grammar and Language Use	4	3	2	1
Uses a range of academic vocabulary appropriate for formal, academic writing and comparative structure				
Maintains consistent use of complex structures and a variety of sentence types				
Uses correct verbs (time frame, markers, form, and subject and verb agreement)				
Uses correct articles, pronouns, and nouns				
Employs hedging markers to qualify claim				
Mechanics	4	3	2	1
Uses correct punctuation with evidence of editing and proofreading				

Total Points (64 possible): ________
Grade (Percentage): ________

Grading Rubric: Commentary

Guidelines	✓
Submitted by due date	
Double-spaced	
Approximately two pages (11-point font)	

Content	Points			
Audience and Purpose	4 (A)	3 (B)	2 (C)	1 (D)
Has clear intended audience				
Contains clear persuasive thesis, reflects unique claim				
Content and Support	4	3	2	1
Includes believable support				
Contains appropriate multi-levels of support				
Uses in-text source signals				
Flow of Information at Macro Structure	4	3	2	1
Includes an introduction and discussion				
Has a title that connects to the thesis and the introduction includes well-mapped ideas or moves				
Contains supporting paragraphs with topic sentences				
Includes a concluding idea with significance, prediction, warning, or call for action				
Flow of Information at Micro Level	4	3	2	1
Employs linking strategies (words, phrases, and punctuation) to connect ideas within sentences and between sentences in paragraphs				
Grammar and Language Use	4	3	2	1
Uses a range of academic vocabulary appropriate for formal, academic writing and commentary				
Maintains consistent use of complex structures and a variety of sentence types				
Uses correct use of verbs (time frame, markers, form, and subject and verb agreement)				
Uses correct use of articles, pronouns, and nouns				
Employs hedging markers used to qualify arguments				
Mechanics	4	3	2	1
Uses correct punctuation with evidence of editing and proofreading				
Total Points (64 possible): ______ **Grade (Percentage):** ______				